What Your Colleagues Are Saying . . .

"Deeply reflective and an absolutely essential tool for educators at all levels! This brilliant and powerfully transformative guide takes us along a journey of learning that includes a deep dive into understanding how our very own story and experiences shape our beliefs and behaviors toward social justice in education."

—Gloria E. Ciriza, Assistant Superintendent,
San Diego County Office of Education

"The authors provide the perfect balance—a guide to self-reflection and a call to action. This is the right guide for the right time. The journey to becoming a social justice educator starts now!"

—Peter Dallas Finch, Superintendent,
West Valley School District

"*Becoming a Social Justice Educator* is a powerful read for anyone hoping to create learning spaces in which all students feel valued and respected. The reflection questions and activities built into each chapter lead the reader on a powerful journey of vulnerability and greater self-awareness. If schools are to be a safe, inclusive space for all students to excel and be successful, we must better understand the impact our experiences have on the system in which we work."

—Amy DeLaRosa, Systems Alignment Specialist,
Kansas MTSS and Alignment

Becoming a Social Justice Educator

Becoming a Social Justice Educator

A Guide With Practice

Zachary Scott Robbins

Dominique Smith

Sarah Ortega

Oscar Corrigan

Bryan Dale

CORWIN

Fisher & Frey

A SAGE Publishing Company

FOR INFORMATION:

Corwin

A SAGE Company

2455 Teller Road

Thousand Oaks, California 91320

(800) 233-9936

www.corwin.com

SAGE Publications Ltd.

1 Oliver's Yard

55 City Road

London EC1Y 1SP

United Kingdom

SAGE Publications India Pvt. Ltd.

Unit No 323-333, Third Floor, F-Block

International Trade Tower Nehru Place

New Delhi 110 019

SAGE Publications Asia-Pacific Pte. Ltd.

18 Cross Street #10-10/11/12

China Square Central

Singapore 048423

Vice President and
  Editorial Director: Monica Eckman

Director and Publisher,
  Corwin Classroom: Lisa Luedeke

Associate Content
  Development Editor: Sarah Ross

Editorial Assistant: Madison Nevin

Production Editor: Tori Mirsadjadi

Copy Editor: Melinda Masson

Typesetter: C&M Digitals (P) Ltd.

Proofreader: Theresa Kay

Indexer: Integra

Cover Designer: Candice Harman

Marketing Manager: Megan Naidl

Printed in the United States of America

Library of Congress Control Number: 2023936079

This book is printed on acid-free paper.

23 24 25 26 27 10 9 8 7 6 5 4 3 2 1

DISCLAIMER: This book may direct you to access third-party content via web links, QR codes, or other scannable technologies, which are provided for your reference by the author(s). Corwin makes no guarantee that such third-party content will be available for your use and encourages you to review the terms and conditions of such third-party content. Corwin takes no responsibility and assumes no liability for your use of any third-party content, nor does Corwin approve, sponsor, endorse, verify, or certify such third-party content.

Contents

Visit the companion website at
resources.corwin.com/socialjusticeeducator
for downloadable resources.

Publisher's Acknowledgments

Corwin gratefully acknowledges the contributions of the following reviewers:

Paula Bourque
Literacy Author and Instructional Coach
Augusta School Department
Gardiner, ME

Lynn M. Angus Ramos
English Language Arts Curriculum Coordinator
DeKalb County School District
Decatur, GA

Introduction

··

We must first acknowledge and agree upon this: diversity, equity, and inclusion can be complex. Schools and the educators in them are tasked with facilitating positive educational and social outcomes for children. That is more likely to happen in schools where community members are treated equitably, and where equitable distribution of resources is a priority, but social justice sometimes gets politicized. The mention of diversity, equity, and inclusion makes some people defensive. We ask that you avoid looking at social justice through a political lens or as something imposed on students to force them to behave in some pre-scribed way. As authors, we all believe students should be free to choose how they see the world. We do not believe children should be told whom to dislike or influenced to shame others in the name of social justice. Instead, we ask readers to consider social justice as this: a community agreement about the fair treatment of everyone and the fair distribution of resources and opportunities.

Ensuring students' schools and classrooms are safe and respect-ful learning environments is not always easy. As a group of authors, we believe that teachers come into this profession to make a difference. Teachers positively impact students' social, emotional, and academic lives. We believe no educator goes into the teaching profession to hold lower expectations for some students, to treat students unfairly, or to emotionally hurt them. That said, we are not naïve. Sometimes, school communities know or strongly suspect their policies, practices, and behaviors negatively affect students.

This is why there is an urgent need for social justice educators. There is a need for educators who see the beauty of diversity, who encourage curiosity about the perspectives of others, and who engage students in dialogue that matters. We understand the importance of an education that is academically rigorous, but also ask that we please ensure that stu-dents see the value they bring to the classroom. We want to ensure that all students realize their personal goals. To support this work, we ask that we all take on the task of ensuring that school resources and opportuni-ties are distributed equitably.

While we understand this may be easier to accomplish in some places than others, we ask that you do what you can to help all students have wonderful, equitable experiences at school. While this book focuses heavily on students and school staff, please keep in mind that students' families and communities also have a role in ensuring that resources are distributed equitably and that all students feel like they belong. When teachers, students, staff, and families work together to reconcile social justice challenges, that collaboration can be a spark that ignites positive change and strengthens a school community.

We wrote this book to serve as a guide to creating positive school and classroom communities. All students' voices should be heard. As part of our content standards, teachers are responsible for teaching students to express themselves through speaking and writing. We can use those opportunities to encourage students to share their ideas and respond to the ideas of others; we must also teach them how to do so. Schools must be courageous enough to allow students to bring their authentic selves to classroom discussions and to comment on school policies that impact them. This requires schools to allow authentic, respectful, developmentally appropriate discussions about privilege and discrimination.

Importantly, such discussions do not aim to make any school community member feel guilty or divide school community members. Rather, these discussions are meant to increase school community members' understanding of each other and of themselves.

This book will ask you to reflect on your personal and professional life and decide what you believe is right and good for children and society. You may find some concepts in these pages that you've never considered before, and the novelty of those concepts might cause you some discomfort. Such discomfort may be a sign of cognitive dissonance—your reconciliation of how you see this book's concepts relative to your experiences. We encourage you to recognize that dissonance and consider the ideas we present as they may allow you to come to terms with your thinking and help you take action.

> *Children should have champions—social justice educators—who ensure that schools are a place of wonder and joy.*

We are a multiracial, gender-diverse group of authors who are members of various communities. For us, exploring social justice concepts together has been a journey of collective self-discovery and an affirmation of the power of schools. We are affirmed in our collective belief that schools must be inclusive, unbiased places for all children. Sadly, while all students should learn in inclusive, fair classrooms where they are encouraged to be their beautifully authentic selves, a cursory look at news headlines about schooling reveals that some students are marginalized and need equal justice, equitable opportunities, and their fair share of school resources.

When Corwin asked us to write this book, we all jumped at the opportunity. There are teachers, school leaders, and a school district superintendent on our writing team. We are excited to share what we have learned about ourselves and our path to becoming social justice educators. Children should have champions—social justice educators—who ensure that schools are a place of wonder and joy. Individually, we have worked hard over the years to ensure that our respective schools are places where every child feels comfortable learning and where students can succeed. We are happy to share what we have learned with you.

In writing this book, our mission has been twofold:

1. To bridge the gap between academic research on practices and policies related to culturally responsive practices and actual classroom practices

2. To support educators in building a more inclusive learning environment for all students

We do not believe there is a one-size-fits-all approach to creating an inclusive learning environment for all learners. Instead, our research leaves room for you to subjectively relate what is in this book to your own experiences and to apply the identified pedagogies, practices, and principles to your classroom in ways that work best for your students.

We are thrilled that you have chosen to join us in reflecting on schooling and the importance of becoming social justice educators. Let's begin.

CHAPTER 1

Know Yourself

. . . .

Honesty and transparency make you vulnerable. Be honest and transparent anyway.

—Mother Teresa

Who am I?

That is certainly a question that has fueled philosophers, poets, scholars, and spiritual leaders across the span of human existence. The quest to understand ourself never ends, partly because how we define ourself changes across experiences. Forging an identity as a social justice educator begins with deepening your understanding of yourself.

It is a common misconception that being a social justice educator requires you to leap in and do something to change others: to change students, colleagues, and systems. Of course, taking action in the name of social justice is important, even noble. However, for those actions to result in the desired outcomes, educators must first be reconciled with their own self-identity—understanding what evokes emotion, awakens passion, and inspires a call to action. What truly matters to you, and what drives your behavior? This first chapter is designed to help you explore your identity.

Becoming a Social Justice Educator

Self-knowledge is foundational to the work of social justice educators. Exploring our own cultural influences and identities gives us insight into the frame through which we see the world—and how that frame also limits our view. The interactions we have with others who have a different frame often lead to misunderstandings between us. And our frame also informs how we perpetuate institutional and structural barriers that continue to do a disservice to children and communities. When others speak of dismantling systemic barriers, we must remember that we are a part of that system—and we may even unconsciously contribute to maintaining it. If we don't first identify who we are as we seek to cultivate a social justice mindset and then adjust our approach as needed, how can we possibly expect others to change?

What's "Culture," Anyway?

Traditional definitions of culture, the ones we learned in school, usually focus on the explicit and implicit patterns of behavior, language, symbols, and values that make groups different. We suppose that definition works in a historical sense, when it describes a geographically isolated group of people who never intermingled with anyone else, but in a world connected by modes of travel and telecommunications, the idea that a person is a member of only one culture doesn't really fit. Think of all the possible cultural influences inside this person:

> A fifteen-year-old cisgender boy growing up in Atlanta loves crunk music, practices his family's religion but has questions, and aspires to be a social media influencer. His parents, both physicians, don't support this dream. His grandparents fled Iran with their daughters in 1979 to escape the revolution. His grandparents speak Arabic. He knows a few words and phrases but has difficulty communicating deeply with them. When he goes with his parents to his grandparents' house, he enjoys *masgouf*, a traditional Iraqi dish. He also loves Mexican American food, especially the fish tacos his boyfriend introduced him to. He and his boyfriend keep their relationship secret from their families; however, they are "out" as a couple at their high school.

Could you ever assign a single "culture" to this adolescent? Our first cultural influences are usually derived from our families, but our perspective and identity continue to transform as we have more experiences and interact with others outside our family. Understanding the frame through which we see the world begins with looking at our own family experiences. How much warmth we experience in a family unit influences how we forge our respective self-identities (Benson & Johnson, 2009). In particular, the amount of conflict we experience among and between our family members—and our predisposition for coping with conflict—influences how we forge our self-identity. We are influenced by how our parents and guardians monitor and control our behavior as children, and how our family treats us in relation to our siblings (Benson & Johnson, 2009).

Families tell stories from one generation to the next, and they immerse us in experiences that make up the fabric of who we are. Almost unconsciously, we identify with the heroes and she-roes of our family stories, and we connect with the comic and tragic figures of these stories. Families preserve and honor their culture through this oral tradition, preserving an intersectionality of culture through their familial biographical narratives.

> *Families tell stories from one generation to the next, and they immerse us in experiences that make up the fabric of who we are.*

These unique narratives communicate how the family beliefs intersect with larger ethnic, racial, and gender narratives, to name a few, as well as the family's collective perspective on social justice issues.

Self-identity does not develop in a vacuum. Your self-identity has developed relative to your interactions with others, especially your family. As you continue your journey into social justice work, you must understand your cultural autobiography and how it influences your decision making.

NOTES

_____

_____

_____

_____

_____

_____

_____

_____

_____

_____

_____

_____

_____

_____

_____

_____

_____

_____

_____

Pause and Ponder

Begin your own cultural autobiography with a reflection about your family of origin or your family of choice. Note that some of the questions may not apply to you, but we encourage you to consider each of them as a potential shaper of your identity.

QUESTION	REFLECTION	HOW HAS THIS IMPACTED YOUR SELF-IDENTITY?
When and where were you born?		
Where did you live between birth and age eighteen?		
Where did your parents or guardians grow up?		
Where did your grandparents or extended family or caregivers grow up?		

QUESTION	REFLECTION	HOW HAS THIS IMPACTED YOUR SELF-IDENTITY?
What events did you celebrate as a family growing up?		
When there was a big decision to make in your family, who participated? Was there anyone who had the final word in major decisions?		
As an adult, how are major decisions in your family made?		
As an adult, with whom do you discuss your thoughts and feelings? Why?		
As an adult, do you discuss your thoughts and feelings with people outside of your family?		

Intersectionality

Our cultural influences emanate from our family experiences, but they certainly do not end there. Our identity is further informed by our race, gender expression, sexuality, ethnicity, socioeconomic status, nationality, citizenship, religion, and ability. This intersectionality of identities is simultaneously political and personal, and it speaks to our relative power (Crenshaw, 1989).

In the late 1980s, Kimberlé Crenshaw's pioneering work on race and gender issues challenged the dominant feminist movement of the time, which was oriented to the experiences of white women but offered little space for Black feminist thought. Crenshaw argued that by failing to see the role race plays in the experiences of Black women, oppressive systems continued unabated. Since that time, her seminal work on intersectionality has informed nearly every aspect of social justice work in legal, economic, and educational movements. Social justice efforts are piecemeal at best when we fail to address how intersectionality impacts discrimination, privilege, and the systemic barriers and affordances that thwart the dreams of some while giving the appearance of ease to others.

The intersectionality of identities means that we cannot separate the death of Breonna Taylor at the hands of police officers without accounting for her race and gender, her socioeconomic status, and her identities as a sister, daughter, friend, and EMT.

Similarly, we cannot understand the Dakota Access Pipeline protests without accounting for the historical traumas of Native Americans. We also have to understand the power imbalance between multinational corporations and the people who live on the land, and the activism of twelve-year-old Tokata Iron Eyes, who started the ReZpect Our Water movement and stated, "They're not the ones being affected. So why should they get to make the decisions?"

Now that you've created a cultural autobiography pertaining to your family history, we'll help you explore the concept of racial identity—your own as well as experiences that have shaped your perceptions.

Racial Identity

The individual and collective experiences of this group of authors led us to want to explore and share our ideas for becoming social justice educators. We explore the current intentional and unintentional biases and practices that impact the social-emotional and academic lives of students. And in doing so, we have discussed the impact these practices have had on specific groups. In that discussion, we have had to use terms to define large groups of racial/ethnic groups.

We have chosen to use the terms *Latino/a* and *Black* for two such groups. As we discuss in this book, the labels and words we choose to represent ideas, concepts, and people are important. We understand that some people would prefer that we use different terms to describe these racial/ethnic groups. We hope that you understand that we are aware of the limitations of the various terms. For example, Oscar and Sarah identify more with their families' countries of origin (Colombia and Mexico, respectively) rather than a broader category that encompasses a larger group of people with a shared language, and presumably shared culture. We also recognize that "shared language" isn't even sufficient to bind these countries together, because Portuguese, French, the Indigenous language of Nahuatl, and many more languages serve as the means of communication from Mexico to the tip of Chile.

In our discussions and writings, we have chosen to use the term *Black* instead of *African American* for several reasons, drawing on a range of personal, historical, cultural, and social factors. Our decision was influenced by the fact that some individuals may prefer one term over another based on their unique experiences and connections to their cultural identity. The historical context of the terms also played a role, as the term *African American* emerged in the late 20th century as an alternative to *Black*. While some individuals might feel a stronger connection to the term *African American* due to its emphasis on their ancestral ties to Africa, others may prefer the term *Black* for its historical significance in the civil rights movement and Black Power movement. Additionally, we recognized that the term *Black* can be seen as a more inclusive, broader racial category that encompasses people of African descent from various countries and cultures. Generational and regional differences also factored into our decision, as preferences for one term over another can vary by age group and geographic location. We considered that some individuals might choose one term over another to make a political or social statement or express solidarity with a particular movement or cause. Ultimately, our choice to use the term *Black* was based on a thoughtful consideration of these diverse perspectives and factors.

We also use the term *Asian American*, but we recognize that many of our colleagues also identify more closely with their family's country of origin. This decision is based on an understanding of the complex interplay of personal, historical, cultural, and social factors that influence individuals' self-identification. For some, using the term *Asian American* provides a sense of collective identity and solidarity that spans various nationalities and cultures within the broader Asian continent. However, we recognize that others may prefer to emphasize their specific cultural heritage and connections to their family's country of origin, as it allows for a more precise representation of their unique experiences and traditions. In this context, generational differences, regional differences, and personal preferences can all play a role in shaping an individual's choice of identification. Additionally, the term *Asian American* may be seen as a way to challenge the "model minority" stereotype and promote solidarity among diverse Asian communities in the United States. By using the term *Asian American*, while also acknowledging the varying ways our colleagues may identify, we strive to create an inclusive and respectful environment that acknowledges the diverse backgrounds and perspectives of those we engage with.

The terms that we have chosen to use are connected to our personal life experiences and backgrounds, but these terms are in no way intended to marginalize or isolate. Instead, our focus is on our shared responsibility to create an educational system that allows all voices to be valued, and spaces to be created for all students to use their unique talents and strengths to leave their positive impact on this world.

Have you ever analyzed the experiences that have impacted your own racial identity?

Have you ever analyzed the experiences that have impacted your own racial identity? Further, have you considered that how we come to know things has implications for racial self-identity and how we think about issues of social justice (Drago-Severson & Blum-DeStefano, 2014)? Constructive developmental theorists say there are four ways of knowing:

▶ **Instrumental.** People with this orientation see the world through a concrete right-or-wrong lens. They engage in little perspective taking.

▶ **Socializing.** People with this orientation hold the belief that there is no one right way to see the world. They engage in more perspective taking relative to personal ideals.

▶ **Self-authoring.** This orientation describes people who value taking the perspective of others to understand their thoughts and feelings, who order these values by importance, and who take action on others' thoughts and feelings relative to their own judgments.

▶ **Self-transforming.** People with this orientation open their thinking and identities to continual reflection and development, and they collaboratively reflect and explore alternatives.

Regardless of how you've come to "know" and see the world, knowing yourself is integral to becoming a social justice educator. We each have to reconcile—and sometimes confront—life experiences we have had and how those experiences shape our attitudes about race and race group membership. When we reconcile the race-based interactions in our lives and how they influence our behavior, we may see that some of our beliefs are in opposition to the goal of behaving more justly to the children whom we teach and to those who teach them. This reconciliation may also reveal beliefs that undermine behaving more justly toward students' families and our colleagues, who are equally responsible for our students' education.

Further, this reconciliation may show us that we aren't always aware of how our belief systems— and resulting behaviors from them—can sometimes be in opposition to and undermine social justice. Understanding this can help us take action and advocate for others, including those who may have identities that differ from our own.

Reconciliation of race-based interactions is one of several important steps in becoming a more socially just educator.

Reconciliation of race-based interactions is one of several important steps in becoming a more socially just educator. We all need to understand our racial autobiographies to more easily identify implicit bias and microaggressions, reduce stereotype threat, and create safe places for our students and colleagues to learn.

All of us have been shaped by our ancestors in some way. Sometimes, that influence is painful to discuss. As an example, Dominique remembers an incident in which his dad, who is Fijian, was stopped by the police in a suburban part of the town where they live. The officer asked where his dad was visiting from and said they didn't get a lot of Black Americans in that part of town. Dominque's dad has driven very cautiously ever since, and he continues to warn his children about their interactions with the police.

Zachary remembers a "community" swimming pool in his hometown that had an unspoken rule: Black people were not allowed to swim there. To swim at that pool, you had to be a "member" of the community organization or get "invited" by a current member to join. The swimming pool was surrounded by a tall fence, and the membership of the community swimming pool seemed to be exclusively white, though the neighborhood where the swimming pool was located was diverse. Zachary saw the swimming pool almost every time he or his family drove somewhere because the pool was adjacent to a major throughway, which was named after the confederate Battle of Big Bethel, one of the earliest land battles in the Civil War. For years, Zachary never saw a person of color inside the gates of that pool.

Both of these types of experiences, and thousands more, shape our views. Unless we analyze them and put them to the equity test, we might think that other people are less than or more deserving than us, depending on our positional power. Again, a good first step to viewing these situations clearly is to use a self-transforming perspective to view these situations and to understand our own racial autobiography.

Pause and Ponder

Start with your racial autobiography bookends.

What can you recall about the earliest and most recent events and conversations about race, race relations, and/or racism that may have impacted your current perspectives and/or experiences?

- Earliest: What was your first personal experience in dealing with race or racism? Describe what happened.

_____

_____

_____

_____

_____

_____

- Most Recent: Describe your most recent personal experience in dealing with race or racism. Describe what happened.

_____

_____

_____

_____

_____

_____

_____

To help you think about the time between your earliest and most recent racial experiences, jot down notes to answer the following questions (adapted from Singleton, 2021). Let the questions guide but not limit your thinking. Note any other memories or ideas that seem relevant to you. When you have identified some of the landmarks on your racial journey, start writing your racial autobiography. Remember that it is a fluid document, one that you will reflect on and update many times as your racial consciousness evolves.

1. **Family**

   ▶ Are your parents or guardians the same race? Same ethnic group? Are your brothers and sisters? What about your extended family (uncles, aunts, etc.)?

▶ Where did your parents or guardians grow up? What exposure did they have to racial groups other than their own? (Have you ever talked with them about this?)

▶ What ideas did they grow up with regarding race relations? (Do you know? Have you ever talked with them about this? Why or why not?)

▶ Do you think of yourself as white? As Black? As African American? As Asian American? As Latina/o? As Hispanic? As Native American? As Indigenous? Or just as "human"? Do you think of yourself as a member of an ethnic group? If so, what is its importance to you?

2. **Neighborhood**

▶ What is the racial makeup of the neighborhood you grew up in?

▶ What was your first awareness of race (that is, when did you realize that there are different "races" and that you are a member of a racial group)?

▶ What was your first encounter with another race? Describe the situation.

▶ When and where did you first hear racial slurs?

▶ What messages about race do you recall getting from your parents or guardians? From others when you were little?

3. **Elementary and Middle School**

▶ What was the racial makeup of your elementary school? Of its teachers?

▶ Think about the curriculum: What African Americans did you hear about? How did you celebrate Martin Luther King Jr. Day? What about Asians, Latinas/os, or Native Americans?

▶ Cultural influences (TV, advertisements, novels, music, movies, etc.): What color God was presented to you? Angels? Santa Claus? The tooth fairy? Dolls?

▶ What was the racial makeup of organizations you were in (Girl Scouts, soccer team, church, etc.)?

4. **High School and Community**

▶ What was the racial makeup of your high school? Of its teachers?

▶ Was there interracial dating? How was interracial dating perceived by the people around you?

▶ Were racial slurs used? Were there conflicts between races?

▶ Have you ever felt or been stigmatized because of your race or ethnic group membership?

▶ What else was important about your high school years, racially speaking (maybe something that didn't happen in high school but during that time)?

▶ What is the racial makeup of your hometown? Of your metropolitan area? What about your experiences in summer camp, summer jobs, and so on?

5. **Present and Future**

▶ What is the racial makeup of the organization you currently work in? Of your circle(s) of friends?

▶ When you think about where you want to live in the future (if that's different from where you are now), what is its racial makeup? Social class makeup? Where do you want to work in the next ten years? What is its racial makeup? Social class makeup?

6. **General**

▶ What is the most important image, encounter, or thought you've had regarding race? Have you felt threatened? Have you ever felt in the minority? Have you felt privileged?

The Power in Names

One of the first of countless decisions parents make is naming a child. They consider things like what the name might rhyme with because of teasing. They consider all the people with whom they have interacted, and when one partner suggests a name, the other thinks about whether it brings up any painful memories. Parents ask themselves if the name has positive or negative connotations, and they contemplate if it represents their culture and family.

This team of authors has a lot of experience with choosing names (five times as of this writing). For example, Dominique's son's name is Nixon. Immediately, people assume that Dominique named his son after the thirty-seventh president of the United States. That can sometimes translate into a false perception of who Dominique and his family might be. Some individuals do not support President Nixon or his values, and they assume Dominique shares those values. This shouldn't happen, but it does. The fact is, there is a watch company based in California called Nixon. It is the watch brand that Dominique wears daily, and each time he looks at his watch, it serves as a reminder to make time for his son.

Small but hurtful interactions can happen often because of a name. Let's take Dominique's name as another example. If you haven't met him or viewed his photo, there is a chance that you might have thought he was a woman because some believe Dominique is a "female" name. Dominique can recall every interaction when someone mispronounced his name after being introduced, calling him Dominick instead. He has no issue with anyone mispronouncing his name initially—that happens. However, he has come to realize that when someone still mispronounces his name after multiple interactions, he checks out of the conversation. Dominique's disinterest in those who appear to *choose* to mispronounce his name doesn't stem from a place of disrespect. Rather, Dominque feels that the other person is not invested in getting to know him. He can also remember every teacher who changed his name because they couldn't get it right. They created *Dominic*, *Dom*, and *D*, letting Dominique and his identity fade away. Instead of trying to change themselves, they chose to try to change Dominique.

This harmful approach happens daily within schools. Students with names that are difficult for speakers to pronounce get nicknames, shortened names, or even completely different names. How many times have we been in this position as a student? How many times have we done this as a teacher? In reflection, have we gotten upset with a student because they were disengaged? Might they have disengaged partly because we kept saying their name incorrectly—perhaps without even realizing it—resulting in a student who didn't feel important?

Nomenclature—what we call things—matters.

How we name things influences how we think about them. The technical term for this is *linguistic relativity* (Lucy, 1997). Josephine Livingstone (2014) reminds us of a central idea from the linguist Benjamin Lee Whorf: "All observers are not led by the physical evidence to the same picture of the universe, unless their linguistic backgrounds are similar." For instance, the images and emotions evoked for Zachary by the words *refugee* and *political prisoner* or from a name such as *Queen* or *Debo* may be very different for people with a different linguistic background or racial socialization than Zachary.

Some may judge the parents and their values based on the names they give children, and others may recognize the tradition of unique names in the Black community (e.g., Logan, 2020). Nomenclature—what we call things—matters. Words generate thoughts, and thoughts are the fertile ground from which behaviors grow. In becoming a social justice educator, you must be conscious of how the names you give to people, places, and things—let alone how you say them—support just behavior and fundamental fairness for all or undermine it.

Pause and Ponder

Your name reflects your identity, and in many cases it tells something about your own origin story. Family members may have told you how you got your name. Were you named for an ancestor or a friend of your parents who meant so much to them? You might have been named after a celebrity or a television character. Or maybe your parents just liked the sound of the name. For example, all of us who have worked on this book have our own stories.

Zachary: Named after the priest and prophet Zechariah in the Old Testament of the Bible

Dominique: Named after basketball star Dominique Wilkins

Sarah: Named after the biblical figure in the Old Testament meaning *princess* in Hebrew

Oscar: Named after fashion designer Oscar de la Renta and salsa singer Oscar D'León

Bryan: Not named after anyone; his mom wanted a name that couldn't be shortened

What's yours? _____

_____

What assumptions do people make about you when they hear or read your name for the first time? Which assumptions are positive? Which are negative? Is there an instance where assumptions based on your name prevented you from doing something? Did your name open a door for you?

_____

_____

_____

_____

_____

_____

_____

_____

_____

_____

_____

_____

_____

The Dominant Culture of Schools and the Ideal of Discourse and Dissent

Schools also have their own culture, and while there are differences between schools that make each one unique, most operate similarly. Schools in the United States tend to privilege an individualistic, competitive approach. (Consider how grades are awarded, honor rolls are determined, and class rankings are reported.) This approach teaches that property is owned by an individual, and the physical world is knowable (Trumbull et al., 2000). Education is framed as a means to become upwardly mobile to create a more materialistically enriched future. (Consider the assumption that all students should strive to attend college.) This agenda has become even more pointed in the last two decades as postsecondary liberal arts education programs close while science, technology, engineering, and mathematics programs grow at high rates (Shamir, 2020).

Schools in the United States tend to privilege an individualistic, competitive approach.

In contrast to these Anglo-Saxon Protestant institutional values of schools, some cultures hold a more collectivist view of the world. Success is defined more often at the group level, and the group's interdependency relies on its members' social skills. This sets some children up for difficulty when they move to the United States from another country and suddenly need to navigate a school culture that is unlike the one they experienced at home. For example, in an article titled "Why I'm Not Involved," Jung-Ah Choi (2017), a U.S. education professor who grew up in South Korea, recounted her dismay and humiliation at her son's kindergarten conference. The teacher told Choi her son was disruptive. As Choi noted,

> I expected to have a conversation with the teacher. I expected the teacher to ask questions about Michael's family life. I expected a true parent-teacher partnership for the benefit of his education. I expected the teacher to take an interest in my approach to raising Michael. But all I heard from his teachers—that year and the next—was information about where he stood on the spectrum from struggling to smart and where he stood on the obedience spectrum (from disruptive to respectful). . . . "Mommy," he told me in kindergarten, "I am in the bad behavior group at school." (p. 48)

Her frustration is well founded. How can teachers know about a child's culture if communication is one way and focused only on the dominant culture of the school?

Social justice educators, administrators, and families should not view the dominant culture of a school as permanent, particularly if that culture does not meet the educational needs of all students. Those who insist on social justice and fair education for all students can dissent when schools fail to meet the needs of students. Schools typically mirror the ideals of a society. Education systems are the vehicle that reproduces societal culture (Mathews & Savarimuthu, 2020).

Marginalized students need social justice champions who advocate for their right to a free and appropriate public education. Social justice educators must find ways to dissent from cultural norms that undermine learning and justice for groups of students. Discourse and productive dissent are fundamental to a democratic society. How else are those governed by policies and laws expected to share their thoughts on how decisions impact them? The framers of the U.S. Constitution institutionalized the ideal of discourse and dissent in the First Amendment when they penned the notion that the public must protest against the state if it behaves unjustly. This protest is defined by discourse and dissent.

Marginalized students need social justice champions who advocate for their right to a free and appropriate public education.

As social justice educators, we cannot be indifferent to decisions or decision-making processes that impact us or the people we care for, specifically our students and their families. We can discuss, share dissenting views, and disagree without being disagreeable. Admittedly, this has not been modeled very well at school board meetings throughout the country, especially during discussions about race, ethnicity, and inclusion. Still, discourse and dissent are fundamental to democratic processes, and the officials who make decisions about schools must balance the interests of the community and the needs of all children. These discussions surface a community's values. Through discourse and dissent in our schools, at school board meetings, and embedded in reporting about education in the news, and through the ratification of education policies, our intersectionality impacts how we decide what's important and what values dominate the culture of our community's schools.

NOTES

Pause and Ponder

How was education discussed in your family? Reflect on the values imparted to you about schooling. Did your school regularly communicate with your family? What were the expectations your school held for your family? Did you experience a difference in values between home and school?

_____

_____

_____

_____

_____

_____

_____

_____

The Rich Points

Social justice educators recognize the profound influence culture and identities have on our perceptions and actions. We are often the product of multiple cultures, rather than a single one. Anthropologist Michael Agar (2006) offered this thought experiment in one of his talks.

What if I . . .

1. went to college in the 1980s rather than the 1960s?

2. were female rather than male?

3. grew up Jewish rather than Catholic?

4. were raised in Mississippi rather than California?

5. were a native speaker of Spanish rather than English?

6. delivered a sales pitch rather than a lecture?

Would any of these differences have been noticed? (p. 3)

Yes, it is highly likely that these differences would have been noticed and would have likely impacted the experiences he had in college. Agar calls this noticing of differences on the part of listeners the "rich points." These rich points include moments of confusion that you may experience when you talk with someone and realize that you don't understand something they have said. They are rich because they hold a wealth of information about both parties. When those rich points occur, you find yourself at a crossroads and must make one of three decisions:

▶ Ignore your lack of understanding and hope you'll reach a point where it makes sense again

▶ Attribute your lack of understanding to a shortcoming on the speaker's part

▶ Wonder why you don't understand and see it as an opportunity to know more about yourself through the other party

Unfortunately, the first two options occur all too frequently. But importantly, the third decision can't happen if you don't have a sense of your own identity and how it impacts and limits your understanding of the world.

Each of us has an intersectionality of identities that inform how we see ourselves and others. Those frames are, at times, highly aligned with others. In those cases, you share a similar background and set of experiences with some people, and your communication with them is effortless. You rarely have those moments of lost understanding. But in other cases, your frame differs from those with whom you interact. This can be especially true if you teach at a school where the students' experiences are not like yours.

Teachers may also experience generational differences between themselves, their students, and their professional colleagues. In fact, generational differences surfaced for us while writing this book. Our author group consists of a Baby Boomer, two members of Generation X, and two Millennials. We learned more about each other through reading each other's writing and examining social justice concepts from our varying perspectives. The diversity of our perspectives provides rich points of insight for us as authors, and we are thankful we can share our thoughts with you. The concepts in this book deepened our understanding of each other and ourselves. We hope you have the same experience.

NOTES

Pause and Ponder

How do you respond when your frame differs from those around you? What is it like for you to explore the richness of those differences? Think of a time when you lost understanding with someone. How did you chase a rich point? Reflect on an interaction you had with someone of a different generation than your own. What was confusing to you? How did you respond to your confusion?

_____

_____

_____

_____

_____

_____

_____

_____

Conclusion

Knowing ourselves requires a self-awareness and a self-consciousness that not only benefit our personal well-being but also shape our ability to impact the social, emotional, and academic learning of students. In our pursuit of becoming social justice educators, we examine how our self-identity has developed. We consider the complexities in the intersectionality of identities, including how racial identities have contributed to our perspectives and our frame of the world. We recognize that our own names and the words we choose as labels for people and ideas matter because of the associated connotations. We encourage the practice of analyzing the dominant culture of the school and its alignment to the values and culture of the students who learn within its walls. As social justice educators, we search for the "rich points" when communicating with students, families, and colleagues so that we can deepen our understanding of others and, in turn, grow our understanding of ourselves.

3-2-1 Chapter Reflection

Take an opportunity to think about the content of the chapter and what it means to you.

- What are three important ideas from this chapter?

_____

_____

_____

_____

_____

- What are two action steps you can take based on this chapter?

_____

_____

_____

_____

_____

- What is one idea or concept you would like to explore further?

_____

_____

_____

_____

_____

CHAPTER

2

Stereotype Threat

The whole idea of a stereotype is to simplify. Instead of going through the problem of all this great diversity—that it's this or maybe that—you have just one large statement; it is this.

—Chinua Achebe

The journey of a social justice educator can be quite complex. This expedition entails many peaks and valleys. It forces us to meet many challenges around ethnicity, race, sexuality, religion, and many more essential issues. We must reflect on our preconceived biases as educators. These biases will interfere with how we treat our students, particularly our minoritized students. Therefore, it is crucial to recognize that if we fail to address the biases that we possess before engaging with our students, we may cause great harm to the students whom we serve.

Left unchecked, our biases can produce a toxic learning environment for our students—one where some do not feel valued, do not feel welcome, and do not experience a sense of belonging. As social justice educators, we must purposely strive to meet the needs of our minoritized students. We must strive to create welcoming learning environments that nourish and celebrate the great diversity that our students have to offer. We can only accomplish this goal by understanding who our students are, including their backgrounds and the many challenges and barriers they face.

One predominant challenge that minoritized students face in schools is stereotypes. Before we continue, consider the range of students who have been minoritized in your own community. Is the discrimination based on race and ethnicity? Religion? Gender and sexual orientation? Poverty? Language learning? What are the demographics and characteristics of students' identities that cause them to be minoritized? The answers to these questions should give us all pause.

Stereotypes can be defined as "an exaggerated belief associated with a category. Its function is to justice (rationalize) our conduct in relation to that category" (Allport, 1954, p. 191). Marginalized students are too often regarded negatively in their schools. As researchers suggest, this approach can be extremely harmful: "Imagine yourself in a situation where the people around you believe you are *not* smart or capable, and they came to this judgment without consideration of your past performance, your motivation to work, or your actual skills and knowledge, but instead based their evaluation on little more than your gender, your age, or even the color of your skin" (Rydell et al., 2017, p. 294). Imagine how it must feel to be regarded as less capable by those around you. Imagine how difficult it must be to succeed under these circumstances. Unfortunately, this might actually be your current situation at work, school, or home.

Pause and Ponder

Think back to your own experiences as a K–12 student. What stereotypes affected you personally? Did those stereotypes play a role in how you felt as a student?

_____

_____

_____

_____

_____

_____

Which stereotypes are used to describe students around you? Which stereotypes do/did you hold about others?

_____

_____

_____

_____

_____

_____

Understanding Stereotype Threat and Its Impact on Students

Social categorization is defined by Hewstone and Giles (1997) as a core cognitive process that involves "the segmentation and organization of the social categories or groups" (p. 271). As they note, the process serves several functions: "reducing the complexity of incoming information; facilitating rapid identification of stimuli; and predicting and guiding behavior" (p. 271). Being categorized into a group—whether it's race, ethnicity, sexual orientation, or gender—tends to be inevitable, so it's important to recognize that our students are impacted by the stereotypes or stigma attached to the group(s) with which they identify. In particular, what happens when these stereotypes affect the academic performance of minoritized students? Claude Steele, an American social psychologist and professor of psychology at Standard University, spent years researching and analyzing the effect of stereotype threat on minoritized student performance.

According to Steele et al. (2002), stereotype threat is a situational phenomenon that members of negatively stereotyped groups experience when they worry about confirming that negative stereotype with their performance. Steele proved that minoritized students underperformed academically because of the pressure related to their constant worry about the stereotype associated with their identity group.

Steele conducted several studies to research the impact that stereotype threat had on the testing performance of African Americans. Steele and Aronson (1995) reasoned that "whenever African American students perform an explicitly scholastic or intellectual task, they face the threat of confirming or being judged by a negative societal stereotype—a suspicion—about their group's intellectual ability and competence" (p. 797). This meant that African American students lost time and cognitive energy by focusing on the perceived stereotype even though they were fully capable of high achievement. Since they were also dealing with the anxiety and the self-doubt associated with stereotype threat, rather than focusing their entire cognitive energy on the assessment, African American students were bound to underperform.

During Steele's studies (Steele & Aronson, 1995), African American and white college students who possessed the same cognitive skills were given a thirty-minute verbal test with components from the GRE. This study was split into three groups, a diagnostic group and two nondiagnostic conditioned groups. For the participants in the diagnostic group, "the test was described as diagnostic of intellectual ability, thus making the racial stereotype about intellectual ability relevant to African American participants' performance and thus preempt any threat of fulfilling it" (Steele & Aronson, 1995, p. 799). For the nondiagnostic groups, there was no mention of intellectual or verbal ability; instead, those participants were told that the purpose of the research was to understand the psychological factors involved in solving verbal factors. As you may have guessed, African American students in the diagnostic group scored significantly lower than those in the nondiagnostic group.

Pause and Ponder

What verbal and nonverbal cues might you be using in your classroom that trigger stereotype threats in your students?

_____

_____

_____

_____

_____

_____

As Steven Spencer and his colleagues noted, "Stereotype threat, it is important to stress, is conceptualized as a situational predicament— felt in a situation where one can be judged by, treated in terms of, or self-fulfill negative stereotypes about one's group" (Spencer et al., 1999, p. 6). Many studies have been done to examine the effects of stereotype threat on diverse social groups. For example, Spencer and colleagues (1999) analyzed the impact of stereotype threat on gender, particularly related to performance in math. A widely held societal stereotype is that women do not perform as well as men when given a difficult exam in math. To test this belief, Spencer and his colleagues set up a two-part experiment in which women and men of equal mathematical skills were given thirty minutes to complete a complex mathematical examination.

At first, the results of the initial study seemed to confirm the stereotype. Both women and men were told that they were taking a math test with two sections. The sections varied in difficulty. One section contained questions requiring higher math levels (such as calculus), and the second section contained questions revolving around lower levels in math (such as algebra). The women and men were given instructions and told that they would receive their test scores upon completing the test. The results showed that women and men scored similarly in the easy section of the test. However, in the challenging section of the test, women scored significantly lower than men. The researchers were puzzled: How could this be? The participants all had equal content knowledge. Why did women score considerably lower?

Their next study proved once again that removing stereotype threat would dramatically affect women's test performance. The testing conditions of the second study remained the same, but this time the participants were told that the test's purpose was to show gender parity in math abilities. The researchers found that "characterizing the test as insensitive to gender difference was enough to totally eliminate women's underperformance in this experiment . . . we believe that by presenting the test as one on which gender differences do not occur, we made the stereotype of women's inability irrelevant to interpreting their performance on the test—this particular test" (Spencer et al., 1999, p. 12). Women in the second study scored at similar levels to their male counterparts. Removing the stereotype threat allowed the women in this study to focus all of their cognitive abilities on taking the test.

Social justice educators ensure that they create learning spaces in which all students feel competent, capable, and motivated to work. While the examples provided earlier refer to African Americans and women, Latino/a, Native American, and Asian American students, as well as members of other social groups, are also affected by stereotype threats. Therefore, we should question how we design our lessons, structure our assessments, and cultivate the environment in our classrooms to make them psychologically safe spaces for all students. Social justice educators ensure that they create learning spaces in which all students feel competent, capable, and motivated to work.

Eliminating the Stereotype Threat

Many studies have shown that stereotype threat has a significantly negative impact on the academic performance of stigmatized groups. As social justice educators, we must all work to eliminate the perceived threats, judgments, and anxiety that students experience, and to create learning environments that allow minoritized students to focus on academic excellence. Next we'll share some teaching strategies that you can incorporate to diminish and eradicate stereotype threat from your classroom.

Building Trust

Julius Green, a high school English teacher, strives to eliminate the stereotype threat from his classroom by creating a culture of trust and emphasizing high academic achievement. He states, "I believe that my students must understand that I value who they are from the moment they come into the classroom." Mr. Green emphasizes the importance of building trusting and meaningful relationships with his students, and he allows his students to feel safe, valued, and respected. As a direct result, Mr. Green has created a learning environment that will enable students to focus solely on their academic progress and achievement.

Jesus, a student in Mr. Green's class, confirms the value of this approach. He explains, "Mr. Green's class is different. I enjoy being in the class because he cares about us. You know, he doesn't just teach. He is always talking to us about our families, our lives, the things we do outside class."

Although Jesus may not recognize it, Mr. Green has found a way to incorporate his students' identity and culture into the classroom. His students understand that he values their past experiences. They feel represented in the classroom, which immediately counteracts any stereotypical feelings they may have regarding their teacher.

But building trusting relationships with students is not enough for Mr. Green; he also expects his students to achieve high academic standards. He says, "I want my students to understand that I expect them to achieve such high standards because they are fully capable of achieving it. Each student is capable of learning. I want them to know that I grade them based on their academic merits."

In Mr. Green's school, the rubrics and assessments are carefully crafted to facilitate and assess learning. We must convey to our students that we believe in their abilities. To eliminate stereotype threats in our classrooms, our students must understand they are being graded fairly.

Isabella Benavides, a second-grade elementary school teacher, also understands the importance of intentionally building positive student–teacher relationships to foster trust in the classroom. Ms. Benavides explains, "Our students have to know that we care about them. Yes, that we care about their academic lives, but [that we care about] their personal lives as well. We care about them as people."

Each morning, Ms. Benavides brings the class together for a morning community circle, and she designs questions to get students to learn about each other, problem solve together, and learn about different perspectives. She takes notes on the children's answers so she can make a point to connect with students later in the day.

An enthusiastic second grader, Christine appreciates this approach. She says, "At lunch, Ms. Benavides asked if she could see my drawing book. I was thinking, 'How did she know I had a special drawing book?' But it's because she remembered that I talked about that in community circle."

Asking students for updates on their personal interests builds a classroom culture that is the foundation for academic achievement. Ms. Benavides expects these second-grade students to engage in learning that is challenging, and her approach helps ensure that they feel capable and motivated to take on the challenge.

Pause and Ponder

How can you build trust in your classroom? In what ways can you eliminate stereotype threat when administering assessments to students?

_____

_____

_____

_____

_____

_____

Representation

Social justice educators can fight against the detrimental effects of stereotype threat in various ways. For example, the impact of stereotype threat can be mitigated by increasing the representation of people from underrepresented groups in highly regarded positions, such as inviting successful community members from various backgrounds into the classroom to give presentations on their careers. The mere presence of members of minoritized groups dramatically reduces the impact of stereotype threat.

Murphy and colleagues (2007) studied the effect of stereotype threat on women in math, science, and engineering settings, and their results provide insight into the importance of representation. They told study participants they were watching videos from a conference on leadership in the sciences, although in fact the people in the video were actors. The gender composition of the discussion groups in the video varied; study participants saw discussion groups that were either predominantly male or gender balanced. Then, researchers asked study participants if a local university should host the fictitious conference based on the discussion in the video they watched.

The researchers found that women who watched the videos of predominantly male discussion groups felt less comfortable attending the fictitious conference than women who watched the videos where discussion groups were gender balanced. Murphy and colleagues (2007) concluded, "when a setting contains threatening situational cues, it raises the specter of identity threat—prompting heightened cognitive and physiological vigilance, decreased feelings of belonging, and decreased desire to participate in the setting" (p. 884). In comparison, the female math, science, and engineering students who watched a gender-balanced video reported feeling a much stronger sense of belonging (scoring a 4.79).

We must make every attempt possible to introduce our students to field leaders representing their social groupings.

What does this study tell us about our own students? Like the women in this study, students are more likely to feel stressed, be anxious, and experience a lower sense of belonging when they feel underrepresented. Therefore, we must make every attempt possible to introduce our students to field leaders representing their social groupings.

Jessica Thibodeau, a high school science teacher, tackles this challenge by introducing her students to the "what does a scientist look like" lesson. She explains, "This is one of my favorite lessons because women and minoritized groups are unrepresented in science. I want our students to see that scientists represent all genders, ethnicities, races, and social backgrounds."

According to Mrs. Thibodeau, when she asks her students to describe a scientist at the beginning of the lesson, they all describe a scientist who resembles Bill Nye the Science Guy—an older person who is male, white, and intelligent. Sadly, most students who belong to a minoritized group do not describe a person who looks like them. It is precisely this type of stereotype that a social justice educator confronts head-on. Otherwise, our students will check out; they won't believe that a position that is held in such high regard is attainable. If our students don't think they can become scientists one day, then why would they invest their time in learning about science? Mrs. Thibodeau teaches her students about scientists who represent diverse backgrounds and social groups. At the end of the lesson, when she tasks students with reflecting on what they have learned, the students all highlight one overarching theme: "Scientists look exactly like us." (See Figure 2.1.)

Figure 2.1   Student Self-Portrait as a Scientist

Similarly, the fifth-grade learners in Amaya Kim's class are greeted each month by a community member, and they have the opportunity to learn about a different career. As one example, Dr. Vanessa Leon pays the class a visit. She is a high school classmate of Ms. Kim and works as a family medicine physician in the area. Dr. Leon shows a picture of herself from fifth grade on the screen and shares, "I grew up in this neighborhood. I went to a school down the street. I was a student in fifth grade, just like you are."

Ms. Kim reflects, "This moment is powerful, because many of my students can see themselves, their culture, their language reflected in Dr. Vanessa Leon."

Fifth-grade student Eloisa wants to be a doctor like Dr. Leon. She says, "Seeing her in my classroom and knowing she came from my neighborhood, it shows me that my dream is possible." Eloisa continues, "She even gave me some advice. She says to always be curious about learning something new. I can do that."

Pause and Ponder

Minoritized groups and women are underrepresented in the field of science. In what other areas are minoritized groups underrepresented? How can we increase the visibility of minoritized people in highly regarded positions or positions of authority?

_____

_____

_____

_____

_____

_____

Student Agency

There is no universal definition of student agency, yet every educator recognizes it when they see it. Students who put forth effort and recognize the impact or outcome of that effort have a strong sense of agency. Students recognize that they are central to the learning process—the decisions they make to put forth effort are part of the determining factor of their success. As noted by the U.S. Department of Education's Office of Educational Technology (n.d.),

> Learners with agency can "intentionally make things happen by [their] actions," and "agency enables people to play a part in their self-development, adaptation, and self-renewal with changing times" [Bandura, 2001]. To build this capacity, learners should have the opportunity to make meaningful choices about their learning, and they need practice at doing so effectively. Learners who successfully develop this ability lay the foundation for lifelong, self-directed learning.

Student agency is malleable and learnable.

Importantly, student agency is malleable and learnable. It's not a personality trait that some students are born with and others are not. As part of their *Future of Education and Skills 2030* initiative, the Organisation for Economic Co-operation and Development (OECD, 2019) noted that student agency requires the "capacity to set a goal, reflect and act responsibly to effect change. It is about acting rather than being acted upon; shaping rather than being shaped; and making responsible decisions and choices rather than accepting those determined by others." Here are the key points the OECD notes regarding student agency:

- Agency implies that students have the ability and the will to positively influence their own life and the world around them.

- In order to exercise agency to the full potential, students need to build foundation skills.

- The concept of student agency varies across cultures and develops over a lifetime.

- Co-agency is defined as interactive, mutually supportive relationships—with parents, guardians, teachers, the community, and each other—that help students progress toward their shared goals.

Research on student agency in schools identified eight dimensions: self-efficacy, pursuit of interest, perseverance of effort, locus of control, mastery orientation, metacognition, self-regulation, and future orientation (Zeiser et al., 2018). Let's briefly look at each dimension in more detail.

- **Self-efficacy.** Students need to believe they can achieve their goals; this conviction is foundational to student agency. Children who possess a higher level of self-efficacy than their peers believe that they can reach goals. Self-efficacy, with an effect size of 0.71, reliably holds the potential to accelerate learning (www.visiblelearningmetax.com).

- **Pursuit of interest.** Think of this as consistency of passion for a topic. Students pursue their interests by reading books, talking with others, practicing, and searching for new challenges that will build their skills. An important aspect is that they stick with some interests for a period of time and don't lose interest quickly (Peña & Duckworth, 2018).

- **Perseverance of effort.** Related to interest is the willingness to continue on when something becomes more difficult. A student's persistence and concentration of effort to finish tasks has the potential to accelerate learning, with an effect size of 0.54 (www.visiblelearningmetax.com). A student with a higher degree of persistence understands that setbacks can happen but is willing to see a project or task through to the end.

- **Locus of control.** The key word is *control*. To what extent do learners believe that they are influencers in the successful completion of the task? Students with a strong internal locus of control place a higher value on their own skills and effort, while those with an external locus of control focus on the difficulty of the project or what other people's skill levels are. An internal locus of control is associated with higher levels of achievement (Shepherd et al., 2006).

▶ **Mastery orientation.** Goals drive all of us, but our motivation to achieve them is also important. The goals of students can fall broadly into two paths: a mastery orientation or a performance orientation (Pintrich, 2003). Students with a mastery orientation understand that what they are learning benefits them, whereas students with a performance orientation want to complete tasks and get the reward (grades, stars, etc.). A student focused on mastery is willing to invest a higher degree of effort. That kind of motivation has an effect size of 0.57 and can accelerate learning (www.visiblelearningmetax.com).

▶ **Metacognition.** Often described as "thinking about thinking," metacognition develops in the first years of schooling and continues across a lifetime. Metacognitive strategies are embedded in instruction. As an example, we teach early readers to monitor their understanding so that when they lose meaning in a text, they can go back to reread. We teach older students to take notes and use them as part of their studying. Students with a higher degree of metacognition will notice what is confusing, ask questions, and mentally summarize what they are learning.

▶ **Self-regulation.** Closely related to metacognition is the self-regulation needed to learn. For example, students with a higher degree of self-regulation can reset their attention during reading when they notice they're thinking instead about a video game. They can monitor their focus and use their tools to regain that focus when it is lost.

▶ **Future orientation.** Perceptions of what constitutes the future vary with age. However, one goal of schooling is to help students see that the learning they do today is an investment in their own future aspirations. Students with a strong sense of agency recognize that their efforts and outcomes influence their future learning as well as their current performance.

The intentional use of teacher practices specifically aimed at building student agency has shown promising results over time, as short as within a single school year (Zeiser et al., 2018). As Figure 2.2 shows, these practices can be organized into three categories: student opportunities, student–teacher collaboration, and teacher-led approaches.

Here's an example of what this might look like in practice. The learners in Natalie Moore's fourth-grade classroom are reflecting on the week. She asks students to demonstrate their understanding of the concepts studied over the last couple days: character analysis and text evidence. Students are allowed to choose how they will demonstrate their understanding. Tyler chooses to complete the weekly quiz, and Anaya chooses to write a short script.

Figure 2.2 Teacher Practices That Support Student Agency

STUDENT OPPORTUNITIES
Choice. Students make choices about aspects of the content and process of their work.
Group work. Students have opportunities to work with peers to learn and practice skills necessary for group success.
Harnessing outside opportunities. Students have opportunities to demonstrate agency outside the classroom and make connections to its application in the classroom.
Revision. Students are encouraged to revise assignments or tests after they receive feedback.
Student self-reflection. Students self-reflect using journals, logs, or other structured templates or tools.
Student-led instruction. Students demonstrate agency by leading instruction on a particular skill or concept.

STUDENT–TEACHER COLLABORATION
Developing relationships. Teachers develop personal relationships with students to better understand their strengths, needs, and motivators.
Feedback. Teachers provide students with feedback and scaffold the process of students seeking feedback.
Goal setting. Teachers help students set learning goals while improving agency.
Individual conferences. Teachers hold one-on-one meetings with students to discuss elements of student agency and its relationship to academic work.
Student voice. Teachers provide students with opportunities to contribute to and provide feedback on key decisions in the classroom.

TEACHER-LED APPROACHES
Assessment. Teachers use tools to evaluate student agency.
Direct instruction. Teachers provide explicit instruction to develop skills related to student agency.
Modeling. Teachers model agency to demonstrate it for students in a meaningful context.
Positive reinforcement. Teachers provide positive reinforcement for demonstration of agency.
Scaffolding. Teachers provide students with tools, strategies, and resources to help scaffold students toward mastery of agency.
Verbal cues. Teachers provide brief spoken prompts in real time to highlight or remind students of behaviors that demonstrate agency.

Source: Adapted from Zeiser, K., Scholz, C., & Cirks, V. (2018).

Ms. Moore explains, "It is important to me that students get to make some choices. Sometimes I provide choice in who students work with and what materials or manipulatives are available, but my favorite way to incorporate choice is to find times when students can choose how they will demonstrate their learning."

Student opportunities for choice promote motivation and give students a sense of ownership and achievement. Anaya mentions that the class learned how to read and write scripts as part of their Readers' Theater fluency practice. She says, "I want to be an actress or write scripts for movies one day, and I like it when Ms. Moore lets us choose how we are going to prove that we learned. Most of the time I pick script writing, but sometimes I write poems." Figure 2.3 is a student example of how content and choice in demonstrating understanding can be merged together to increase student ownership.

> *Student opportunities for choice promote motivation and give students a sense of ownership and achievement.*

Figure 2.3   Character Analysis Script

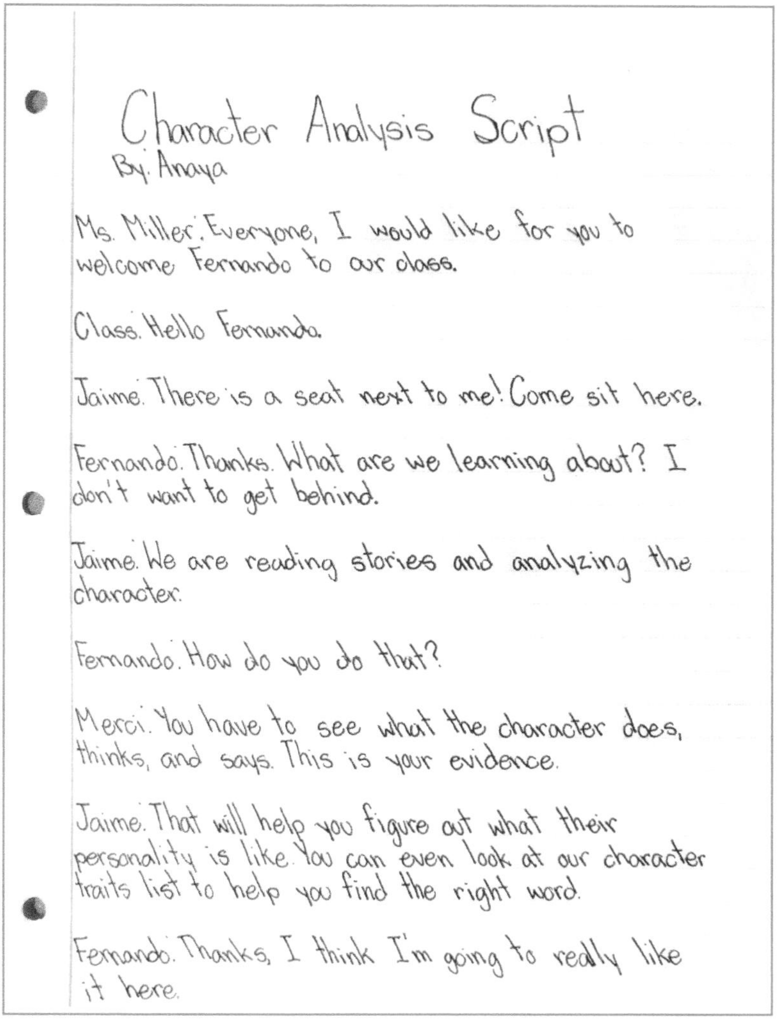

Character Analysis Script
By: Anaya

Ms. Miller: Everyone, I would like for you to welcome Fernando to our class.

Class: Hello Fernando.

Jaime: There is a seat next to me! Come sit here.

Fernando: Thanks. What are we learning about? I don't want to get behind.

Jaime: We are reading stories and analyzing the character.

Fernando: How do you do that?

Merci: You have to see what the character does, thinks, and says. This is your evidence.

Jaime: That will help you figure out what their personality is like. You can even look at our character traits list to help you find the right word.

Fernando: Thanks, I think I'm going to really like it here.

Pause and Ponder

Which teacher practices in the categories of student opportunities, student–teacher collaboration, and teacher-led approaches do you use to support student agency?

_____

_____

_____

_____

_____

_____

_____

_____

_____

_____

_____

_____

_____

Conclusion

Negative stereotypes are prevalent throughout our schools. As social justice educators, we must be willing to stand and fight against these stereotypes. Introducing teaching practices that build our students' trust and agency can help eliminate the detrimental effects that stereotype threats have in our classrooms. Better yet, we can help ensure that students believe in their learning abilities, are prepared to succeed in settings outside of school, and are confident that they can attain highly regarded positions as adults.

3-2-1 Chapter Reflection

Now take an opportunity to think about the content of the chapter and what it means to you.

- What are three important ideas from this chapter?

  _____

  _____

  _____

  _____

  _____

- What are two action steps you can take based on this chapter?

  _____

  _____

  _____

  _____

  _____

- What is one idea or concept you would like to explore further?

  _____

  _____

  _____

  _____

  _____

Implicit Biases

> We can at least *try* to understand our own motives, passions,
> and prejudices, so as to be conscious of what we are doing when
> we appeal to those of others. This is very difficult, because our
> own prejudice and emotional bias always seem to us so rational.
>
> —T. S. Eliot

Our jobs as educators provide us with a unique opportunity to interact and participate in the growth and development of young people of diverse backgrounds. The methodologies we use to teach content standards, directly and indirectly, impact the quality of students' learning experiences worldwide. To ensure that schools benefit all students, educators must value every student's uniqueness, meet students where they are academically and socioemotionally, and do all they can to help students be academically successful.

Social justice educators must also be aware of how implicit biases nuance the dynamics of interactions with individual students, the classroom, and the greater community. When educators acknowledge and work toward removing the unconscious attitudes and stereotypes that exist in us all, schools are better suited to provide high-quality education for all learners.

Solely being aware of our own unconscious biases will not change schooling for students; we must also identify institutional and structural barriers to high-quality teaching and learning, and then take steps to develop anti-biased policies and procedures to dismantle them. In other words, we must be conscious of implicit bias and make material changes to how schools work.

Implicit Bias

Let's address the elephant in the room: we all have biases. A long time ago, our ancestors used bias (e.g., "insider" versus "outsider") to make split-second decisions about who was friend or foe. Then, as our society, living conditions, and brains matured, humans co-opted the use of biases as cognitive shortcuts to simplify our workloads. We create mental scales to weigh—disproportionately—in favor of or against certain ideas, opinions, purchases, interactions, friends, and so on. (The list could go on forever.) The point is that bias is not all bad. Often, we use bias in a positive way to help navigate the ever-busy day we experience as teachers (and humans). For example, we often assume that taking a highway will be quicker than taking a back road without actually taking the time to actually check traffic conditions. Unfortunately, our shortcuts can also lead to a deficit mindset, narrow-minded stereotypes, and overgeneralizations that can have a negative impact on the students and communities we serve. These mental processes can happen unconsciously within our brains' complex and hidden mechanics.

Your Brain on Bias

Our brains are hardwired to find patterns and associations to help us make sense of our surroundings. We exercise this cognitive process at an early age. For example, as children we recognize patterns and features that distinguish us from other groups: friendships based on age, sex, gender identity, hair color, classroom teachers, and so on (Baron et al., 2014). As children, we believe that what is similar to us is "good" and what is dissimilar is "bad"—and, therefore, actively disliked (Aboud, 1988; Cameron et al., 2001). Then we practice and hone the skill of seeking patterns and shortcuts, identifying groups, categorizing things, forming opinions, and fearing the unknown. Unfortunately, what begins as a fair and historically appropriate skill can easily develop into a collection of implicit biases.

Implicit Bias Defined

Implicit bias describes the attitudes and beliefs outside our conscious awareness and control. In fact, our implicit biases can oppose our conscious beliefs so indiscernibly that we are often unaware these unconscious beliefs even exist (Greenwald & Krieger, 2006). For example, we may express an explicit acceptance of a specific social group while unconsciously acting in biased ways against that group, such as when people state that they support and embrace all faiths but complain about greeting cards that say *Happy Holidays* instead of *Merry Christmas*.

> Implicit bias *describes the attitudes and beliefs outside our conscious awareness and control.*

To better understand implicit bias, it is helpful to look at our cognitive functions. The mental process behind our cognitive functioning can be placed into two parts: System 1 and System 2 (Kahneman, 2011). System 1 is responsible for the cognition that occurs outside our conscious awareness. These functions happen automatically and are extremely quick. For example, let's say you are waiting at a crosswalk. The red hand is shining across the street from you, so you know to wait. When the pedestrian indicator appears, you know to proceed across the crosswalk. The speed and efficiency of System 1 allows you to associate these arbitrary shapes and colors with meaning, and this requires little to no conscious effort or thought (Staats, 2016).

Conversely, System 2 is where our conscious processing exists. System 2 is used for mental tasks requiring concentration, such as reading a textbook, solving a math problem, or planning a lesson (Staats, 2016). Rather than functioning with the automaticity of System 1, System 2 requires thoughtful work and effort. Together, these two systems help us navigate the world. We are inundated with an innumerable amount of information every second, and most neuroscientists agree that the vast majority of our cognitive processes occur outside of our conscious awareness (Miller, 1956).

Because so much of our cognitive process exists within the associations found in System 1, the quick, snap judgments we make with our unconscious mind may include harmful biases that can hurt others in substantial ways. The most egalitarian of individuals, whose well-intentioned aims are to treat others fairly, can still unknowingly act in ways that reflect implicit bias. Implicit biases are activated by any number of identities we perceive in others, be it race, ethnicity, gender expression, sexual orientation, ability, appearance, or age (Greenwald & Krieger, 2006). Its impact is seen in health care, in the justice system, and in education.

> *Implicit biases are activated by any number of identities we perceive in others.*

Let's look at an example. Like many teachers across all content areas and grade levels, third-grade teacher Rebecca Foley experiences a heavy workload and high demands, a common situation that often creates a work environment ripe for the influence of implicit bias. When those biases form, they can result in lower academic expectations. Ms. Foley's teaching philosophy and personal belief is that all her students can succeed, but unconsciously, she holds her students of color to lower expectations.

Unknowingly, implicit bias has affected Ms. Foley's behavior, specifically when she neglects to give Alejandro, one of her Latino students, corrective feedback about errors in his writing. Although she gives Alejandro a grade, she doesn't identify and address his misspellings and grammatical errors, because she unconsciously believes that he isn't capable of doing the same level of work as others. Consequently, Alejandro is a victim of her implicit bias. Because he has not received the same educational opportunities as his white peers, he is left at a disadvantage. His teacher's implicit bias hinders him from reaching his full potential.

Pause and Ponder

Consider the characteristics of implicit bias and reflect on your current knowledge of each.

1 = I am new to this knowledge.

2 = I am actively learning about this.

3 = I can teach others about this.

CHARACTERISTICS OF IMPLICIT BIAS			
	1	2	3
Implicit bias is pervasive: We all possess implicit bias, even those of us dedicated to being impartial, such as educators.			
Implicit bias is a mental construct: Our brains are hardwired to look for patterns and shortcuts when it comes to decision making and the interactions we engage in with others.			
Implicit bias does not necessarily align with our declared beliefs: Our profession is full of well-intentioned individuals committed to providing all students a fruitful education. While we may outwardly state support of, and consciously celebrate, all social groups, our implicit bias can cause harm to students.			
Implicit bias tends to favor our own ingroups: We tend to connect with and give preferential treatment to people that we perceive to be in the same group. We can also hold implicit biases against our own ingroups (those with whom we share characteristics).			
Implicit bias is a behavior: Our brains are complex; we process massive amounts of information with every passing second. The implicit biases formed from the associations, patterns, and shortcuts we create over time can be gradually unlearned through consistent use of the debiasing techniques.			

Impact of Implicit Bias in Education

Being an educator doesn't protect us from possessing implicit biases—or explicit ones, for that matter. Teachers are society members, and we are subject to societal influences that shape biases. A large study that compared educators to noneducators on measures of explicit and implicit racial bias (specifically anti-Black/pro-white biases) indicated that "teachers' bias levels are comparable to those of the general population whether or not demographic factors among teachers . . . are considered" (Starck et al., 2020, p. 281).

Implicit bias typically manifests in circumstances where individuals are more likely to rely on their unconscious System 1 associations. These include the following (Bertrand et al., 2005):

▸ Situations in which there is ambiguity or incomplete information

▸ Circumstances that include the perception of time constraints

▸ Conditions in which our cognitive control may be compromised because of fatigue or cognitive overload—having too much on our mind

On any given day, teachers encounter many—if not all—of these conditions, and the need to rely on unconscious processes happens naturally throughout a busy day. It is not unreasonable to assume that holding implicit biases—a behavior we all possess—may contribute to the actions and decisions we implement within our classrooms, schools, and learning communities.

Educators rely on established patterns and shortcuts to navigate our classrooms' nuanced environments. As we attempt to organize the typical lively buzz of a learning environment, we build lesson plans, modify curriculum for our classrooms, and implement best practices gleaned from professional learning sessions. But what happens when we encounter a situation we are unprepared for? What implicit biases do we end up drawing upon when evaluating student work? What shortcuts do we rely on when we are presented with an unruly student who does not match the schemas we have developed through experience and training?

Our behavioral response is to default to the patterns and shortcuts we have developed throughout our lives: those attitudes and beliefs that occur outside our conscious awareness—the implicit biases that exist in us all. We enter this profession with an unwavering desire to provide students of all social identities with the most fruitful of experiences. Still, given unknown situations, our execution of such desires can be tainted with harmful actions fueled by our implicit biases.

Implicit Bias and Discipline

Typically, most school disciplinary actions result from daily classroom interactions between students and teachers (Romero, 2018). Research shows that Black students, Latino/a students, students with disabilities, and LGBTQ+ students receive more disciplinary actions and referrals for subjective offenses like defiance, disruption, or disrespect than their white peers do (Girvan et al., 2017; Gregory & Roberts, 2017; Skiba et al., 2011; Welsh & Little, 2018).

Gilliam and colleagues (2016) studied the degree to which racial bias influenced preschool teachers' expectations of classroom behavior. They noted that African American students were more likely to be suspended from school starting as early as preschool. They studied the eye-gaze patterns of preschool teachers as they watched videos of four young children:

a Black boy, a white boy, a Black girl, and a white girl. The researchers told the teachers that the study was intended to determine how educators detect challenging behavior before it becomes problematic. They found that participants of all races spent more time watching the two boys than the two girls, and the most time watching the Black boy, even though the Black boy did not exhibit problematic behavior. Black preschool teachers dwelled on the Black boy at somewhat higher rates than white teachers. It is important to note that, in fact, there were not any problematic behaviors from any of the children in the videos.

Disproportionate disciplinary responses in schools can negatively impact students' development. Social justice educators must remain mindful of these potential impacts and be prepared to mitigate them with appropriate care, concern, discourse, and dissent from policies or actions that undermine the just treatment of all students.

> *Disproportionate disciplinary responses in schools can negatively impact students' development.*

Students of marginalized social groups who receive disciplinary responses more frequently than their white peers too often get tracked in schools and school districts. Teachers too often hastily identify so-called troublesome behavior patterns and assign negative labels to students after one or two minor incidents. This contributes to a cycle of disproportionate disciplinary responses, because people tend to justify implicit bias by searching for validation that the biases are true.

Pause and Ponder

Let's return to the study of racial bias and its influence on preschool teachers' expectations of classroom behavior. The eye-gaze patterns of teachers tracked the Black boy at a higher percentage when looking for potential behavior problems. If you were in the study, what do you think your eye-gaze pattern might have been? In the classroom, do you think that you look for "problematic behavior" more from certain students?

_____

_____

_____

_____

_____

_____

_____

_____

The Case of Jayla

A school was tagged with graffiti one evening. School administrators arrived the following morning and were shocked to find a large letter *Y* with elaborate graphics spraypainted on a wall near the school building's entrance. The administrators immediately associated the act with gang activity. Mr. Zamora, the principal, interviewed six Black students he thought might be involved, including a young woman named Jayla. The principal had negative associations, albeit unconsciously, about the youth in the primarily Black neighborhood near the school, and he associated darker skin tones with criminal behaviors. Though no criminal charges were ever filed, Mr. Zamora determined that each of the six students would be suspended for three days to discourage additional vandalism.

Jayla told school administrators she was home cooking dinner for her younger siblings at the likely time of the vandalism, but her statements were ignored. Jayla, who had never been suspended before, was angry when she discovered she would receive Fs on the assignments she would miss during her suspension; she feared the suspension would harm her chances to attend college in the future. When Jayla returned to school the following week, she felt frustrated and disheartened by the amount of work she needed to do to make up for what she had missed.

Jayla's English teacher, Ms. Davis, held her own implicit biases related to the perception of anger in the emotionality of her Black students. Ms. Davis perceived Jayla's frustration and disheartenment as aggression. Subsequently, she reprimanded Jayla verbally to "change her attitude," missing the opportunity to refer Jayla to a school counselor to help her cope with her feelings about her suspension or how Jayla was expressing her frustration. Oftentimes, the perception by teachers that Latino/a and Black females are "loud" intersects both their gender and racial identities (Caraballo, 2019). In this case, Jayla's teachers and her school failed to create an emotionally safe space for her, which reinforced institutional inequities.

NOTES

Pause and Ponder

Do you know the discipline statistics for your school, district, and state? Examine the discipline data for the most recent school year for which discipline data are available. What are the student groups' rates of suspension and expulsion? Are the suspension rates proportional to student enrollment data? Who appears to be the most likely to be issued a suspension based on the data you found? What efforts are underway to address (or prevent) disproportionality in exclusionary discipline outcomes? Can you identify any gaps or oversights in these efforts?

QUESTIONS	REFLECTIONS
Which student groups are disproportionately represented in your school's discipline reports?	
Which student groups are disproportionately represented in your district's discipline reports?	
Which student groups are disproportionately represented in your state's discipline reports?	

QUESTIONS	REFLECTIONS
What are the current efforts to address disproportionality at your school?	
What are the current efforts to address disproportionality in your district?	
What are the current efforts to address disproportionality in your state?	
What gaps do you see in these efforts?	

Confronting Our Bias

When a dominant group's implicit biases appear in institutional policies, students and educators who are negatively impacted by these biases sometimes suffer additional difficulty. Sometimes that suffering is quiet, and the disparate impact of unfair policies in practice is virtually invisible. That suffering can be palpable in other circumstances, and the evidence of unfair treatment can be jarring. Lack of attention to fundamental fairness often motivates those who believe in social justice from comfortable seats of passive resistance into full-fledged action.

Do not underestimate the impact of the cognitive dissonance we all experience when we believe we are behaving in a just way and then realize how hurtful our behavior is to others. That recognition of cognitive dissonance is akin to the sound of a metal fork running across a glass plate. The epiphany of finally seeing our unconscious, unintentional bias can be disorienting—even disturbing—for educators. Few of us intend to be a source of pain to others, especially when we believe our behavior is in alignment with principles of justice and equity. To reconcile the dissonance, some people lean into their discomfort and engage in self-reflection. Others avoid this self-reflection and resist engaging in discussions about equity and implicit bias. Needless to say, we recommend the former and not the latter.

Resistance to conversations about implicit bias compounds its potential for harm.

Resistance to conversations about implicit bias compounds its potential for harm. When we are uncomfortable with explorations into our behavior and potential biases, we tend to avoid discomfort by steering the discussion in another direction. We quickly bury the issue, smothering self-reflection. We push these conversations back into the individual and collective subconscious depths. However, as social justice educators responsible for educating all children, it is not wise for us to wait until we read the next news headlines that prompt a discussion about race. Before those news headlines are printed, we must engage in the work of reconciling our racial identities, our cultural identities, our identities as educators, and the intersectionality of these unique groups' memberships.

If we are to engage in this work authentically, we must become comfortable talking about it. We must be comfortable discussing how our personal biases influence our work in schools and our efforts to help marginalized students achieve. These conversations become easier once we accept there is no one way to have these discussions, and we don't have to be perfect at having them before we start. Suppose we can look at implicit bias through an institutional lens as well as a personal one. In that case, we can support each other and take action together to question systemic barriers that impede students from reaching their potential. Then we can dismantle those barriers together.

As we have noted, confronting our biases also requires the granular work of gaining self-knowledge. This level of awareness serves social justice educators well.

Pause and Ponder

Exploring and exposing our own potential biases can be uncomfortable. Which statement best describes your status on this journey? Which statement has described you in the past? Also, feel open to creating a statement that more accurately matches your thinking.

☐ I don't believe I have any implicit biases that impact student learning.

☐ I try to steer conversations away from this topic because it is uncomfortable.

☐ I used to think I didn't have any implicit biases, but now I believe I need to reflect more on this idea.

☐ I am in the process of understanding my own culture and identities so I can begin to uncover my biases.

☐ I am actively confronting my personal biases and how they are impacting my teaching and the opportunities provided in my classroom.

☐ I am actively engaged in dismantling systemic barriers at our school site.

☐ _____

Gain Awareness

Objective measures exist that help educators and school communities understand the presence and impact of implicit bias. The Implicit Association Test (IAT) is a tool that has been widely studied and used to gauge implicit bias. The IAT was developed in 1995 by Greenwald and Banaji to measure people's beliefs and attitudes they are unable or unwilling to report toward people in various demographic groups. Since 1995, the original IAT has expanded to include tests on gender, age, race, skin tone, sexuality, religion, ability, and weight. The test identifies the degree to which the test taker associates social groups with evaluations (e.g., good, bad) and stereotypes (e.g., beautiful, dangerous). Variations of the IAT have been administered thousands of times, and the resulting data are free and publicly available. The Race IAT is one of these variations, and it has been found to reliably identify unconscious associations (Nosek et al., 2005). There are now fifteen IATs available, and each takes less than ten minutes to complete.

Tests such as the IAT increase the participants' awareness of implicit bias; they can help us understand that bias is deeply embedded within our mental programming. Gaining an awareness of our implicit biases is an important first step to changing the behavior that is rooted within them.

Pause and Ponder

Take at least three of the IATs available from https://implicit.harvard.edu/implicit/takeatest.html. The Race, Disability, and Sexuality IATs are a good place to start. What did you learn about yourself? What was surprising? What was confirming?

_____

_____

_____

_____

_____

_____

_____

_____

Take Action

Learning about implicit biases can be disconcerting, especially if we believed we had no biases or that we did not allow biases to impact our decision making. Fortunately, when it comes to taking action to deepen our understanding of others, two categories of behavior have been found to reduce our implicit biases. The first is expanding our shared group memberships (Scroggins et al., 2016). The second is learning about diverse people and cultivating acquaintances and friendships outside of our group. Both of these actions can help reduce our implicit biases toward others.

Think about the students you connect with the most. What are your shared experiences and identities? How do those shared experiences and identities impact your ability to form relationships and develop attachments? Consider those students with whom you have tried to forge a connection but have had little success. What role might implicit bias play in your relationship-building processes with these students? What are the perceived differences between you and these students, and how can you bridge those differences? Create opportunities for conversations to happen by initiating meaningful discussions with students about their lives, and be intentionally empathetic in the formative stages of your relationships with these students.

Pause and Ponder

Which of the following action items would you like to pursue? Which action items would push your thinking and learning forward to ensure that you build stronger relationships with all students and positively impact the quality of students' learning experiences?

☐ Make friendships with individuals outside of your group or get involved in a different group.

☐ Engage in conversations about social issues.

☐ Read books (fiction and nonfiction) to learn about different perspectives.

☐ Watch documentaries about social justice topics.

☐ Follow social media accounts that promote social justice topics.

☐ Join a book club.

☐ Make a conscious effort to avoid snap judgments and decisions.

☐ Take three IAT assessments or introduce these assessments in your professional learning community.

Push "Pause" When You're Cognitively Overwhelmed

As we have noted, implicit bias is more likely to influence our decisions as educators when we have incomplete information in a situation or when we feel overloaded, fatigued, and pressured (Bertrand et al., 2005). Be mindful of when you are experiencing fatigue or emotional overload so you remember to push the proverbial pause button.

Figure 3.1 includes some additional suggestions for how to respond in common school situations so you can take the time to check for possible implicit biases before they influence your actions. What ideas can you add?

Figure 3.1 Responding to Implicit Bias

SITUATION	POSSIBLE RESPONSES
A Black student asks about homework that they missed due to an absence just as you are about to begin class.	• Take advantage of opportunities to nurture relationships. When a student does something that causes you to react negatively, take a step back, talk to them, and listen openly to their side of the story. • Acknowledge the student's concern and make a plan with them to follow up before the end of the class period. • Develop an action plan for how you can build positive relationships with students. The act of writing puts you in an active role, consciously planning new actions you can take, and it creates new connections in your brain about how you can behave.
A white parent sends you an email saying that he needs to speak with you immediately because of an incident that occurred after school.	• Prioritize meeting with the parent. Reflect on your practices. Do other parents or guardians receive the same treatment? • Discuss your reflections with a colleague.
You've been grading essays at home for hours, and your family members are asking when you'll be done.	• Recognize that the pressure you are feeling can cause you to rush through the grading process and accept or expect less from certain students. • Give yourself permission to end the marathon grading session. Return to your grading rubric with fresh eyes to finish the job the next day.
The chairperson for the district Pan-Asian Parent Committee contacts you about a comment made in class.	• Check yourself for assumptions you may be making in advance of the meeting. These might be assumptions about parents or guardians in general, about Asian Americans, or a combination of both. • Listen to the concerns voiced in the meeting. Ask clarifying questions to learn more about the perspectives and experiences of others. • Follow up on concerns at the school. Report these to the chairperson as well.

SITUATION	POSSIBLE RESPONSES
A colleague at the school who sponsors the Gay–Straight Alliance asks for time for a student presentation at the next staff meeting.	• Listen carefully to the club sponsor about the details of the proposal. • Ask about the outcomes the club hopes to achieve. • Make a plan for a follow-up session with the staff about taking action. • Use this opportunity to meet with other student leaders about giving them a voice and a forum for sharing their knowledge.
A female chemistry teacher voices concerns in a parent–teacher organization meeting that she is the only woman in the science department, and that there are no people of color.	• Meet with the teacher to learn about her experiences and concerns. • Voice support for her perspectives. • Learn about recruiting and mentoring underrepresented people on the teaching staff.
A male student who identifies as Indigenous is about to be suspended from school for the fourth time this school year.	• Seek to understand the anxieties that contribute to student misbehavior. These may be related to the student's identity and feeling unsafe in the school environment as a result of that identity. • Investigate other teachers' stories of how they used misbehavior to build positive relationships. • Continue to refine your understanding and application of restorative practices.

Conclusion

Uncovering the unconscious seems nearly impossible at first. How do we address the thoughts and beliefs that we didn't intend to have or even know are there? First, we acknowledge that we all have bias, and that the patterns and shortcuts our brain creates can lead to unconscious differences in expectations we hold for students. As educators, we can be aware that we are more likely to revert to acting on these biases under certain circumstances, such as when we feel pressed for time or when there is ambiguity in criteria. There are debiasing techniques such as the ones described in this chapter that we can intentionally engage with to support our work in becoming social justice educators.

3-2-1 Chapter Reflection

Now take an opportunity to think about the content of the chapter and what it means to you.

- What are three important ideas from this chapter?

  _____

  _____

  _____

  _____

  _____

- What are two action steps you can take based on this chapter?

  _____

  _____

  _____

  _____

  _____

- What is one idea or concept you would like to explore further?

  _____

  _____

  _____

  _____

  _____

Microaggressions

I've learned that people will forget what you said, people will forget what you did, but people will never forget how you made them feel.

—Maya Angelou

The idea of microaggressions is essential for all educators to understand because we cannot change what we cannot see, and we cannot see what we do not know to be there. As you continue to reflect on microaggressions after completing this chapter, keep in mind that the first step is consciousness, followed by a new level of mindfulness and sensitivity in your thoughts, words, and actions.

In the process of understanding microaggressions, including their impact on those who use them and on those who are victims of them, it is natural to experience discomfort, resistance, or even both. Seeing ourselves in a new light—whether as a user or as a victim of microaggressions—is challenging. However, it is essential for us to develop this awareness so we can create individual and systemic change, as well as lay the foundation for fair experiences for everyone in our schools. Understanding microaggressions is a key step in bringing our teaching practice and interactions in schools to a place where we choose only words that empower, hold all students to the same standards of rigor and civic engagement, and help students recognize the benefits of greater inclusivity, empathy, and compassion.

This chapter is designed to reinvigorate teachers' dedication to words and actions that positively influence how students view themselves and their abilities. When our words and actions affirm and validate the experiences of our students, they feel safe, valued, and included, which increases their potential for learning. In contrast, microaggressions have the exact opposite effect, leaving targets of microaggressions feeling threatened, excluded, and disconnected from the larger group. Let's examine how to identify them and how to stamp them out.

Microaggressions Defined

Microaggressions are transient daily verbal and nonverbal interactions that convey subtle insults or disparaging messages about an aspect of an individual's race, ethnicity, gender, ability, or other elements of identity. These subtle behaviors—whether conscious, intentional, or unconscious—are directed at members of marginalized groups, and they have a derogatory effect. Initially, the term *microaggression* was coined by Chester W. Pierce, a Black professor of psychiatry at Harvard, to describe the casual insults regularly perpetrated by non-Black people on Blacks (DeAngelis, 2009). Whether expressed in words, body language, or actions, microaggressions are offensive, disrespectful, and hurtful because they communicate an attitude of condescension toward others.

In classrooms, microaggressions occur when teachers consciously or unconsciously express negative or disparaging attitudes or beliefs about students based on the teachers' assumptions about the students' backgrounds and identities. The word *unconscious* is a key component of this chapter. Perpetrators of microaggressions often do not know that their behavior is hurtful to others. It is essential to develop this awareness in order to facilitate change.

The Case of Citlali

To further illustrate the construct of microaggressions, we will begin with an example that is relatively straightforward and tremendously important for building positive relationships with students. Consider the following scenario: A student presents herself as Citlali, but the teacher is uncertain of how to pronounce her name. Which response would help the student feel most welcome and safe in her interactions with the teacher?

Option A: "Wow, your name is really hard to pronounce."

Option B: "You have such a unique and beautiful name. I might pronounce it wrong; you'll have to forgive me."

Option C: "I really want to learn to say your name correctly. Could you say it for me one more time? It's nice to meet you, Citlali."

The best response the teacher could give is option C, because this statement conveys the teacher's genuine interest in and care for Citlali. It is not unusual, however, for teachers to make comments similar to options A and B, with the sole intent of making conversation or forging the initial stages of connection with the student. Unfortunately, these comments communicate a different message. The student may interpret the teacher's message like this: "Citlali's name is not important enough to me to make an effort to learn to say it correctly." Even though the teacher is not speaking these words explicitly, therein lies the disparaging message that makes comments like those in options A and B microaggressions.

Option B is a particularly important example to dissect. Generally, it seems like the teacher wants to interact positively with Citlali; the teacher compliments her name and politely anticipates having trouble pronouncing it. Furthermore, the teacher's comment is unmistakably "nice," but therein lies the problem with microaggressions: they can masquerade as seemingly sensible things to say because the microaggressor is completely unaware of any inherent harm in their statements. In this case, the negative impacts of this comment lie within what isn't said: the underlying message is that Citlali is different in a way that her teacher doesn't value. Instead of including the student's difference, the teacher will not try to learn about Citlali's language to pronounce the name correctly. Yet Citlali, a Latina student in a U.S. school, is certainly expected to learn and pronounce all her teachers' and peers' names. The comment becomes an exclusionary act, and the message—"you are different"—starts to sound more like "you are less than" others.

Microaggressions tear down students and rob them of their agency and identity.

Figure 4.1 provides dimensions of microaggressions as illustrated by the interaction between Citlali and her teacher. Consider how each facet of Citlali's experience of this microaggression contributes to her cumulative day-to-day experiences as a student in a school that operates from the lens of a dominant culture. Microaggressions tear down students and rob them of their agency and identity rather than empower and build students up.

Although this is one instance, consider how many times Citlali may have encountered teachers and other adults who disregarded aspects of her identity because those aspects didn't appear within the adults' linguistic lens. The impacts of repeated microaggressions are a fairly recent topic of study among researchers, but evidence already shows that they have an incredibly profound negative impact on students' psychological and physical well-being (Berk, 2017). It is not far-fetched to imagine the negative mindset that students can internalize when the systemic and pervasive messaging they receive in their academic and social environments repeatedly discriminates against them and quietly labels them as deficient, dysfunctional, or disadvantaged.

Figure 4.1   A Breakdown of the Definition of Microaggressions

TERM	DESCRIPTION	EXAMPLE: MISPRONOUNCING CITLALI'S NAME
Transient	Brief, short-lived encounters	*The interaction lasts only for a moment.*
Daily interactions	Endured on a regular basis	*The teacher says the name incorrectly on a daily basis.*
Subtle	Slight, muted	*The act is not overtly rude; it may even be unintentionally rude.*
Verbal or nonverbal	Communicated through words, actions, body language, or the environment	*The interaction is spoken.*
Disparaging messages	Belittling attitudes or comments	*The underlying message is that Citlali's name is not important enough for the teacher to make the effort to learn it correctly.*
Calling out any aspect of an individual's identity	Race, languages, religion, familial status, age, education, sexual orientation, ability, gender, heritage, geographic location, immigration status, etc.	*Citlali's name is given a different status than other students' names as a result of the language it originates from.*

Types of Microaggressions

Unfortunately, the scaffolds that our brain unconsciously relies on to make decisions about our speech or actions can lead us into ugly situations that harm others. Microaggressions often stem from our unconscious and implicit bias: the attitudes or stereotypes that affect our understandings, actions, and decisions in an unconscious manner. Because microaggressions are often reflexive and unconscious, the individuals who perpetrate them most likely do not even realize they are conveying negative messages.

As the example of Citlali and her teacher shows, microaggressions are more than just insults, insensitive remarks, or inappropriate behaviors; they are a specific form of verbal or nonverbal assault that happens casually, frequently, and, at times, without the intention of causing harm.

Microaggressions can manifest in our verbal and nonverbal actions and are perceived as sexist, racist, hateful, or offensive to marginalized groups. To better understand and identify this form of unconscious bias, let's break down microaggressions into three categories: microinsults, microinvalidations, and microassaults (Sue, 2010).

Microinsults

Microinsults are the most ambiguous of the three types of microaggressions. Microinsults convey rudeness and a lack of sensitivity toward an individual's or group's identity.

Examples of Microinsults

- Asking BIPOC colleagues if they gained acceptance into a prestigious graduate school with the help of affirmative action

- Assuming that female students are not interested in science or mathematics

- Pointing out that an individual's skin color, hair, manner of speaking, or behavior is surprising given their race

- Expressing low expectations for students as a result of the region or part of town where they live

Microinvalidations

Microinvalidations are subtle insults that exclude and communicate a dismissive attitude toward another individual's personal experience. In other words, microinvalidations signal to the victims that their feelings or experiences regarding issues of race or identity are not relevant (Sue et al., 2007). Microinvalidations are ambiguous in nature and involve the assailants denying their own personal racism, homophobia, or sexism (Solorzano et al., 2000; Sue et al., 2008).

Examples of Microinvalidations

- Making statements such as "I don't see color; I treat everyone the same"

- Minimizing the racial experiences of a Black acquaintance by sending them gifts or money during a period of cultural commemoration in the Black community, such as Martin Luther King Jr.'s birthday, Juneteenth, or Black History Month

- Telling a Latina student she is being too sensitive when she advocates for the inclusion of nonwhite authors in next month's book club

Microassaults

Microassaults are closely related to the overt "old-fashioned racism," where the assault is delivered consciously and blatantly and the intention is to cause mental or emotional harm (Malott et al., 2015; Torres et al., 2010). Regardless of the delivery of a microassault (verbal or nonverbal), the intent of the speech is undeniably clear.

Examples of Microassaults

▶ Making statements such as "You're pretty for a Black girl"

▶ Saying "Queer" when a student who identifies as bisexual walks by

▶ Telling a female student that she needs to dress like a girl if she wants to get a date

▶ Using humor that targets a marginalized group

Pause and Ponder

Take a look at one or more of the following videos. What do you see in these videos? What types of microaggressions are evident?

- Fusion Comedy. (2016, October 5). *How microaggressions are like mosquito bites: Same difference* [Video]. YouTube. https://www.youtube.com/watch?v=hDd3bzA7450&feature=youtu.be

- MTV. (2014a, July 17). *Look different: "How'd you get into that school?"* [Video]. YouTube. https://www.youtube.com/watch?v=WXRjO28F_0g

- MTV. (2014b, July 17). *Look different: "Your English is so good"* [Video]. YouTube. https://youtu.be/05BRBKfdDXc

_____

_____

_____

_____

_____

_____

_____

_____

How Do Microaggressions Impact Our Work as Educators?

Microaggressions insidiously work against an educator's efforts to create conditions for productive social, emotional, and academic engagement. Any circumstance that would cause a student to feel personally humiliated, ashamed, enraged, or attacked has no place in a school environment, which should be safe and nurturing for all students.

Teachers need to acknowledge that membership and participation in a dominant cultural group can skew their point of view, attitudes, and dispositions. This bias is largely subconscious until it is serendipitously or intentionally called into consciousness, meaning that even the kindest, most well-intentioned individuals have the potential to commit microaggressions if they lack awareness. It is essential, then, for educators to cultivate their understanding of microaggressions, not only to align themselves more closely with the lens of a social justice educator, but also to promote that same awareness and intentional inclusivity in their students.

Microaggressions Can Hurt Students

Microaggressions have real, long-term impacts on students' psychological well-being (Berk, 2017; O'Keefe et al., 2015) that extend to their academic and social engagement at school. The cumulative experience of perpetual exposure to covert racism, whether intentional or not, can communicate to students that one or more aspects of their identity are inconvenient, burdensome, or inferior to others. This messaging can cause students to develop an internal script that precipitates a negative academic mindset or low engagement in the classroom. Microaggressions can instill a sense of self-doubt and self-hate within students, forcing learners to believe they have little to contribute to the academic community. Microaggressions can also lead learners to believe they are "less than" the dominant classroom group. As a result, these students may be cut off from positive feelings toward themselves and limited in their potential for positive interactions with teachers and peers. Unsurprisingly, microaggressions have been linked to serious mental health concerns, including depression and an increased risk of suicide (Berk, 2017; O'Keefe et al., 2015).

> *Microaggressions can instill a sense of self-doubt and self-hate within students.*

Microaggressions Can Damage Classrooms

When microaggressions are perpetrated in the classroom, the trust that is paramount to the cohesiveness of an educational environment gets challenged. Though microaggressions manifest from an unconscious place

Pause and Ponder

Using the categories of microaggressions, describe why each type of microaggression causes harm to the student.

COMMENT/ STATEMENT	WHAT TYPE OF MICROAGGRESSION IS THIS?	WHY IS IT HARMFUL TO THE STUDENT?
With a tone of surprise, a teacher comments to a Latino student, "You speak English very well."	Microinsult	
A student with a learning disability asks the teacher for additional help and is told if they would just study and try harder, they would be more successful.	Microinvalidation	
A unit exam is scheduled during a religious or cultural holiday observed by a student.	Microinsult	
A teacher facilitates a reading of *Huckleberry Finn* and requires students to say the *N* word out loud in the presence of Black students.	Microassault	
A teacher does not ask English learners any verbal reasoning questions.	Microinsult	

COMMENT/ STATEMENT	WHAT TYPE OF MICROAGGRESSION IS THIS?	WHY IS IT HARMFUL TO THE STUDENT?
A teacher says "I don't see color" to a student who is from a nonwhite group.	Microinvalidation	
A teacher talks with students about the teacher's efforts to support antiminority (hate) groups.	Microassault	
A teacher uses ethnic slurs with students based on their racial, ethnic, or cultural identity.	Microassault	
A teacher ignores a student comment made during class discussion although it is blatantly homophobic.	Microassault	
A teacher says that the Nineteenth Amendment gave women in the United States the right to vote but doesn't mention that it was only white women who were enfranchised.	Microinvalidation	

and impact marginalized individuals through subtle verbal and nonverbal actions, the impact of such an attack can feel extremely tangible. Students on the receiving end of microaggressions are disempowered, implicitly told that their diversity is a burden or unwelcome, and isolated from their peers—leaving them cut off from an invaluable network of friendship, support, and social learning. Microaggressive behavior toward students who don't identify with the dominant cultural group can lead to students being marginalized in classrooms and schools, which undermines teaching and learning.

Microaggressions affect every student who bears witness to them, even those not on their giving or receiving end. Through microaggressions, students are implicitly taught that people are to be grouped socially based on whether they belong to the dominant class or the "other class." This lesson internalizes bias and promotes a belief that students from the "other class" are disadvantaged, at a deficit, less competent, immoral, or unintelligent. This negative paradigm, promoted by microaggressions, can lead to an inhospitable classroom environment where heterogenous grouping is impossible and peer-to-peer interactions are limited to segregated pairings—such as Latino/a students with Latino/a students, Black students with Black students, and LGBTQ+ students with LGBTQ+ students—that reflect a lack of trust and a troubling sense of disconnection among students.

Identifying Microaggressions in Our Teaching Practices

Becoming aware of our own microaggressions often requires humility, first and foremost. It also requires reflection, which may briefly lead us to see ourselves in an unflattering light, but it is not necessary to linger in the mirror for too long. With our attention directed toward teaching and empowering our students to the best of our ability, we can initiate an honest dialogue with ourselves and our colleagues. Here are some exercises that can help.

Exercises to Increase Awareness of Microaggressions in Your Teaching Practice

▶ Keep track of how often you call on and validate all students. Look for trends. Which students do you positively interact with the most? The least? Why is that? What can be done to increase positive interactions so that all students benefit equally?

▶ Monitor the expectations you have for students. Do you lower expectations for some students based on their identities or perceived hardships?

▶ Pay attention to how students carry themselves in your classroom and how they react to your communication. Do they appear uncomfortable or relaxed?

▶ Scan the room to take the emotional temperature of each student. Which students do you see connecting with one another (laughing, speaking, engaging)? Which students are less engaged? Why is that?

▶ Create a survey and ask students questions about how safe they feel taking risks in the classroom, if they feel their teacher believes in them, and so on.

▶ Partner with a colleague to take turns observing each other's students and practices. Share your observations and generate ideas to address areas of growth.

NOTES

Pause and Ponder

Create a microaggression inventory by considering your teaching practice and the practice of your school site. Can you identify instances when these microaggressions appear?

EXAMPLE OF MICROAGGRESSION	WITHIN MY PRACTICE	WITHIN MY SCHOOL SITE
1. Pronouncing a student's name incorrectly, even after they have corrected you		
2. Scheduling assessments/due dates on religious or cultural holidays		
3. Ignoring religious traditions		
4. Focusing on (or engaging/validating) one gender, class, or race of students while ignoring the rest		
5. Requiring students to "represent" the perspectives of a different race, gender, or other aspect of identity in class discussions or debates		

EXAMPLE OF MICROAGGRESSION	WITHIN MY PRACTICE	WITHIN MY SCHOOL SITE
6. Conveying heteronormative metaphors or examples in class		
7. Categorizing the gender of any student based on your opinions or traditional gender norms		
8. Believing all students have access to and are proficient in the use of computers and applications for communications about school activities and academic work		
9. Praising nonwhite students on their use of "good English"		
10. Requiring people with hidden disabilities to identify themselves in class		
11. Ignoring student-to-student microaggressions		

Alter Microaggressive Behavior

Developing your understanding of microaggressions and recognizing how you use them are essential first steps to making impactful changes to your teaching practice. What follows that preliminary work is the intentional unlearning of old habits to make room for more affirming ways of interacting with students. The strategies described next indicate specific attitudes and actions that you can begin working toward immediately. Each strategy aims to show empathy and sensitivity and eliminate the use of microaggressions by placing students' perspectives and empowerment at the center of your attention.

- Be vigilant of your assumptions about students and question the validity of those assumptions as you become aware of them.

- Replace assumptions with positive presuppositions—language that assumes students are making their best effort.

- Provide opportunities for students to develop positive personal narratives about their identities through reflection and authentic discussions.

- Share with students the process through which you developed your unique perspective.

- Model a strong sense of identity for students, including how to assert their perspective when treated with insensitivity and how to demonstrate respect for perspectives that differ from their own.

- Employ materials that represent diverse perspectives, including (but not limited to) all of the perspectives present in the classroom.

- Do not assume students are accustomed to anything you may consider to be a given academic, social, or behavioral norm.

- Do not designate students as spokespersons for their entire group (ethnic, racial, sexual orientation, gender, etc.).

- Share your understanding of microaggressions with students, and facilitate an open dialogue about the topic.

Let's look at another classroom example. First-grade teacher Linda Clark is teaching a science lesson on the different parts of a plant and the parts that help the plant to survive. She begins to get frustrated with a student who continually calls out during the lesson. The student's comments are on topic, but Ms. Clark is exasperated with the child's constant interruptions.

Later, Ms. Clark reflects, "I had to remind myself not to make assumptions based on my perception of this student's motivation for calling out. I mean, from one perspective this student was being disrespectful, but if you think about it some more, this child was engaged and attentive. This child was searching for a more collaborative learning experience."

It is true that a mainstream model for student–teacher interaction is that the teacher provides information, then students listen and respond after being called upon. But in some cultures, a more collaborative back-and-forth exchange is valued. This illustrates one of the actions you can take to affirm student identities: do not assume students are accustomed to anything you may consider to be a given academic, social, or behavioral norm.

Do not assume students are accustomed to anything you may consider to be a given academic, social, or behavioral norm.

Repairing and Responding to Microaggressions

If and when students have the courage to let you know they were offended by a remark or action, listen to them without being defensive; increase understanding through dialogue. Affirm the students' point of view, letting them know that they are seen and heard. Listen and seek to understand the impact of the microaggression on the students, rather than trying to explain your intent.

In addition to being vigilant of our assumptions and repairing microaggressions that we have unintentionally committed, we must develop strategies for responding to microaggressions between students. Consider these scenarios, which show appropriate responses to different microaggressions.

▶ **Scenario 1**: Inquiry

- One student suggests that a statement made by a character in a book is insulting to Black women, and another student states, "That's not offensive. It's true!"

- Your response: "I understand that you disagree with _____. But can you explain to me what you mean?"

▶ **Scenario 2**: Reflection through paraphrasing

- A white student says, "I don't understand why we always have to talk about race. It's not always about race."

- Your response: "It sounds like you are concerned and frustrated about the topic of our discussion. What is it that concerns you most?"

▶ **Scenario 3**: The use of "I" statements

- A student responds to a comment with "Does your mom know you're gay?"

- Your response: "I did not find that comment funny. Please remember our class norms and be respectful of each other."

▶ **Scenario 4**: Redirection and reframing

- When asked a question about terrorism, a student suggests that another student, who is wearing a hijab, would be better able to answer the question.

- Your response: "She can decide if she would like to comment. But I'm interested in the perspectives of all students in this class so that we can think about this topic together. Many groups have engaged in terrorism over the years. Can anyone provide me an example of this?"

Pause and Ponder

Reframing situations you have experienced helps you plan for improved responses in the future. It's worth the time to revisit some situations that are not sitting well with you so that you are more comfortable with responding next time. To begin, identify situations where you felt your language toward others could have been more thoughtful and less microaggressive. Given your knowledge from this chapter, how would you reframe your response in those situations now?

SITUATION	YOUR INITIAL RESPONSE	YOUR IDEAL RESPONSE

It's inevitable: as humans we are fallible creatures, and, given enough time, we will unintentionally insult our students. When that occurs, it is important to acknowledge what you did and strive not to do it again. One way to address this is to design a classroom climate that practices the virtue of humility. It is crucial that you—the teacher—acknowledge that despite all of your best intentions, you might make transgressions or not be fully aware of the circumstances or the impact of your words and actions, and you hope that students will feel comfortable letting you know when they feel slighted or offended. The important thing is to be reflective and open to change.

Conclusion

Microaggressions are "micro" in that they are subtle in nature, but they are massive in the damage they cause. The three types of microaggressions—microinsults, microinvalidations, and microassaults—can be conscious or unconscious, verbal or nonverbal. All of these harmful behaviors attack an aspect of a person's identity, and they strike against the mental health, sense of belonging, and self-worth of the learners in the classroom. When we work to understand our microaggressions and make a concerted effort to change, we are choosing inclusivity and student empowerment.

NOTES

3-2-1 Chapter Reflection

Now take an opportunity to think about the content of the chapter and what it means to you.

- What are three important ideas from this chapter?

  _____

  _____

  _____

  _____

  _____

- What are two action steps you can take based on this chapter?

  _____

  _____

  _____

  _____

  _____

- What is one idea or concept you would like to explore further?

  _____

  _____

  _____

  _____

  _____

CHAPTER 5

Participatory Asset Mapping

A brave man acknowledges the strength of others.

—Veronica Roth

Deficit thinking is a barrier to becoming a social justice educator. When we focus on all the things students cannot do and blame them for their situations, we lower our expectations and fail to focus on aspirations and how education can create change. Yes, many students have lives that do not resemble ours or our upbringing. But pity will not help; in fact, it's harmful. There is a difference between sympathy and empathy. What students need is respect, high expectations, and support to reach those expectations. The approach must start with a focus on assets and strengths. In doing so, we mobilize opportunities for students to learn.

Let's look at a fictional example to see what deficit thinking can look like and why it must be changed: "This is a stressed community I work in," says third-grade teacher Karla Delgado. "Families don't have much, and kids don't have lots of experiences. They don't go to museums or cultural events. Most of them have never been to the beach just ten miles from here. They're all English learners. And they just don't want to learn."

Ms. Delgado is communicating a profoundly damaging deficit mindset that undermines student learning. Deficit thinking is a product of victim blaming, where students are viewed as responsible for "their own internal deficiencies" (Baker, 2019, p. 107). These are manifested in statements that attribute the failure of the school to the following sorts of assumptions, prejudices, and judgments about students and their families (Valencia, 2010).

- ▶ My students have limited intellectual abilities.

- ▶ My students have linguistic shortcomings.

- ▶ My students lack the motivation to learn.

- ▶ My students and their families are involved in immoral behavior.

Asset mapping is the practice of identifying and drawing upon the cultural strengths and community resources that students bring to the classroom. An education that defines students by their perceived deficits will never disrupt systems that perpetuate opportunity and achievement gaps. And it's essential to recognize that these systems don't just operate at the state, district, and school levels; individual classrooms function as microsystems. Deficit-based education does a disservice to teachers, too, as it prevents them from drawing on the tools they need to advance learning—namely, their students' individual and cultural assets (Kohli, 2009).

Asset maps are widely used in cartography as visual representations of the tangible resources of a community. If you have gone on a walking tour of a neighborhood using a map that illustrates where to find public art, festivals, libraries, and historical sites, then you have used a type of asset map. However, cultural asset mapping casts a wider net to identify the physical and intangible assets. These intangible cultural assets include the traditions and stories of the community, as well as the relationships that make a place unique. This approach evolved through work with Indigenous peoples to empower residents. Urban planners and community developers work closely with residents to create a foundation for the vision of a project that preserves and capitalizes on these assets.

NOTES

Pause and Ponder

Cultural asset mapping begins with you. Consider the strengths and cultural assets that have informed your development, both personally and professionally. You began this work with your cultural autobiography in Chapter 1. Review the insights you uncovered, and build on them now. Borrero and Sanchez (2017, p. 283) use these seven questions to help educators frame their personal cultural maps; you can too.

QUESTION	YOUR REFLECTIONS
What are your cultural assets?	
What/who/where has helped you achieve your successes?	
Where do you go for support?	
What led you to become a teacher?	
What/who/where helps you grow and learn?	
What is your cultural history?	
What stories are a part of your culture?	

Make It Participatory

Far too many children hold a false belief that to succeed academically, they must abandon their communities. This belief is reinforced by systemic messages of oppression that communicate the deficiencies of their culture and neighborhood. Therefore, they see school as disconnected from the things they love most: their families, their experiences, and their values (Nieto, 2002). When school is uncoupled from the community, children must make an untenable choice: leave and succeed, or stay and psychologically (and, in some cases, physically) withdraw from education.

Knowledge of students' cultural assets is crucial to gather and use. Students also need to know that what they bring to the classroom is honored and celebrated in the context of schooling. Participatory asset mapping invites students to discover for themselves what they possess.

As part of the process, teachers learn about the assets the students bring to the classroom, enabling educators to leverage their students' strengths better. Importantly, the students learn about themselves through this process. The following sections describe specific steps you can take to help them do so.

Begin With a Physical Asset Map

Young children love to learn about their neighborhood. They are venturing out more with adults, learning mapping skills in social studies, and developing spatial reasoning in mathematics. Older students are also expanding their range as they move about more independently. Capitalize on the relevance of knowing the physical neighborhood by beginning with a physical asset map.

Start with questions that get students thinking about their community differently. One study, which used children to conduct asset mapping in the Alexander First Nation community in Alberta, Canada, began with this simple prompt to elementary students: "Let's say you have a friend coming to visit you in Alexander. It's their first time in Alexander. What would you show them? Where would you hang-out?" (DyckFehderau et al., 2013, p. 4). High school students in the same study took photographs of places to create a visual map of the area to illustrate the traditional map of the community further. See Figure 5.1 for an example of their work.

Figure 5.1 Physical Asset Map Created by the Youth in Alexander First Nation

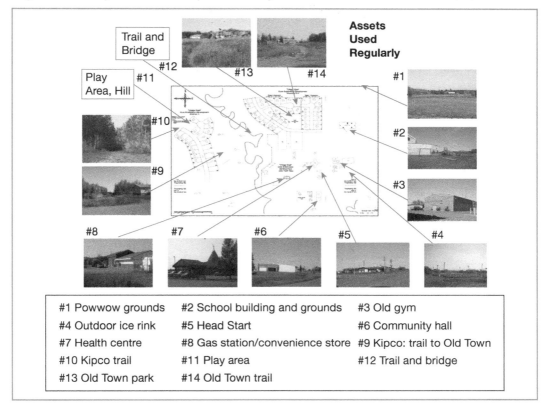

#1 Powwow grounds | #2 School building and grounds | #3 Old gym
#4 Outdoor ice rink | #5 Head Start | #6 Community hall
#7 Health centre | #8 Gas station/convenience store | #9 Kipco: trail to Old Town
#10 Kipco trail | #11 Play area | #12 Trail and bridge
#13 Old Town park | #14 Old Town trail

Source: Dyckfehderau, D., Holt, N., Ball, G., Community, A., & Willows, N. (2013).

Another method for creating a physical asset map is to have students identify places on a large map of their neighborhood using colored dots. To accomplish this, you can lead them through the worksheet in Figure 5.2 one category at a time, and invite them to place the corresponding colored dots on a large map of the community. This map might be a commercially produced one or one that has been hand-drawn on poster paper. As the students affix the colored dots, engage them in a class discussion about the location details. For instance, you might ask how long they have been going to that site or how often.

Figure 5.2 Physical Asset Map Organizer

Where do you and your family go to do these things? Write the location in the second column, then use your colored dot stickers to put it on our map.		
Grocery shopping		YELLOW
Shopping for other things (not food)		ORANGE
Outdoor fun		RED
Seeing a doctor		GREEN
Seeing a dentist		BLUE
Having fun with your friends or family		PURPLE
Going out to eat		PINK
Worship		BROWN
Additional location: ____________________		

online resources Available for download at **resources.corwin.com/socialjusticeeducator**

Pause and Ponder

How well do you know the community where you teach? Conduct your own preliminary asset mapping during nonschool hours by visiting locations your students have identified. Then consider these locations. Are there places you visited for the first time? What were your observations about each location? Who uses it?

TYPES OF ASSETS	LOCATION	OBSERVATIONS	WAS THIS YOUR FIRST TIME VISITING?
Grocery shopping			
Shopping for nonfood items			
Outdoor recreation			
Medical services			
Dental services			
Places where people socialize			
Places where people eat out			
Places of worship			
Other public gathering places			
Other: _____			

Mapping the Intangibles: Cultural Mapping

The next phase of asset mapping is to help students identify the strengths they bring through their cultural traditions, values, and stories. As with the physical map, a major outcome is for students to develop a visual map of themselves. One way to do so is to develop your own cultural map to model for the class. Using the questions in the first Pause and Ponder in this chapter (page 77), develop a set of visuals that represent who you are. For example, if you work with younger children, you can assemble ten meaningful items representing yourself, your family, your community, and your cultural history. Take a photo of yourself surrounded by these objects and write a narrative of what each item represents. Then share this with your students and invite them to create their own asset map. These asset maps must be developmentally appropriate, and the teacher must be aware of the resources available to students. Younger children may gravitate toward selecting their favorite toys, so it can be useful to involve families in helping their children locate objects that represent not only themselves but also their family, community, and culture.

Before introducing the cultural asset mapping project to her students, sixth-grade teacher Pearl Jackson engages students in several activities, readings, and reflections. For example, students complete a family or community member interview, participate in a jigsaw activity about types of thinking, investigate individualistic versus collectivist cultures, and present projects on ancient civilizations. Each activity supports students in exploring how their cultures are sources of strength and integral to their educational lives. As they complete different assignments and projects, the students in Ms. Jackson's class use a graphic organizer (Figure 5.3) to capture ideas that they will later use when creating their personal cultural asset map.

Ms. Jackson notes, "Students have so many strengths that they can draw from, but they don't always realize it. Sometimes they don't realize it because our schools have failed to place value on all students' experiences and cultures. At the start of the school year I design lessons that simultaneously work towards state standards, but also support students as they identify and explore their cultural assets." Ms. Jackson's students are building awareness of themselves so they can draw upon these sources of strength as the cognitive workload increases throughout the school year. Further, Ms. Jackson is learning information about her students that she can leverage to make connections and strengthen her relationships with students. Figure 5.4 shows an example of the organization tool students use to collect notes and ideas to prepare for the cultural asset map project. Figure 5.5 is a cultural asset map created by a student. It is important to note that the student created a bank of ideas and was able to choose those ideas that they felt most comfortable and passionate about.

Figure 5.3 Organizational Tool for Cultural Asset Map

CULTURAL ASSETS AND SOURCES OF STRENGTH	EXAMPLE
Family Members/ Community	
Ancestors	
Adversity	
Talents/Abilities	
Religion/Beliefs	
Traditions	
Strategies for Managing Stress	
Other Assets or Sources of Strength	

online resources Available for download at **resources.corwin.com/socialjusticeeducator**

Figure 5.4 Student Organizational Tool for Gathering Information on Cultural Assets

Cultural Assets and Sources of Strength	Examples
Family Members/ Community - *hospital* Ms. Paloma	mom - single mom — always there for me — can talk to her — good advice → civil rights movement
Ancestors / History *history / mix beauty of is Sadness + strength*	Mexican · African·American · Irish — Mesoamerica · African queen rulers ? — indigenous civilizations · Queen Amanirenas — pyramids (Kush) · fierce + engineering fair
Adversity	— civil rights movement — personal: not ready to talk about it
Talents / Abilities	· bike riding · social / socially aware · creative / artistic · baking — creative "panza llena corazón contento"
Religion / Beliefs / World View	☥ and chakras — combination of — unsure about critical thinker and collectivist or creative thinker individualist ?
Traditions	· piñatas · 3 reyes magos and · Christmas rosca
Strategies for Managing Stress	· baking, riding, baths
Other assets or sources of strength	· circle of friends ♡ — No es suficiente a aprender a montar, también debes aprender a caer.

Using a graphic organizer to assemble and group information is an intermediary step to writing and speaking. It is important for the insights gained from this project to be shared with others. One option is to host a gallery walk for students to view each of the cultural asset maps completed by their classmates. Each student displays their photograph or poster and written summary for the others to view. After completing the gallery walk, host a class discussion about what they have learned about their classmates and themselves. Don't distance yourself from this conversation—share what you have learned about them and yourself too. There are other options for sharing student learning. Some classes may decide to present the information as a speech or recorded video. Figure 5.6 shows a cultural asset map that was created through a presentation program. Each student created one slide and presented a three-minute prerecorded speech to accompany the slide.

Figure 5.5   Student's Cultural Asset Map

Figure 5.6   Cultural Asset Map Presented on an Online Platform

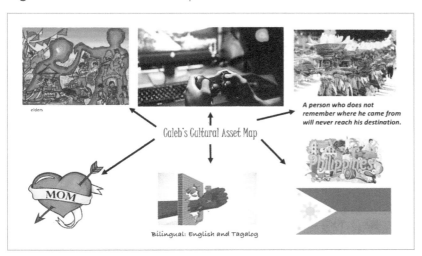

Extend the cultural asset project further by involving families. Instead of a conventional Back to School Night, which more often than not is a one-way communication forum where the teacher talks and families are expected to listen, use your students' cultural asset projects as a means to broker rich discussion and interaction. Depending on the developmental stage of students and the resources available at the school, cultural asset maps can include written summaries, photographs, recorded videos, objects from home, or hand-drawn illustrations. Arrange for students to host their own stations and invite families to talk with their children and others about what each has learned. In their study of elementary and middle school asset mapping, Borrero and Sanchez (2017) noted that "family involvement as a part of the map-making and the gallery walk were crucial parts of the project and served to build a sense of community that included students, parents, and teachers" (p. 290).

Pause and Ponder

Think about the process of cultural asset mapping. Reflect on the benefits to individual students, the class community, and the teacher. Consider ways that you can incorporate cultural asset mapping into the classroom. Also consider how you can create experiences for students to explore their cultural strengths.

_____

_____

_____

_____

_____

_____

_____

_____

Oral History and Cultural Asset Mapping

An important part of our students' assets are the stories they bring with them from their families and community. However, in some cases, they may not be fully aware of what those stories are. As an extension of the cultural asset mapping project, have students conduct an oral history interview with a relative or a community member. Introduce interviewing as a skill and ask students to practice with a classmate. Students can then interview a person of their choice to learn more about their family history or community.

A list of sample oral history project questions can be found in Figure 5.7. However, these should only be a starting point. Brainstorm other questions that might be more aligned with your teaching purposes and the developmental levels of your students. The product of the interview might be a poster or other artistic representation, a video recording of the subject, a written biography including a connection to the student's life, or an oral presentation.

Figure 5.7   Sample Interview Questions

Here is a series of questions that you can use when interviewing a family member or community member. This serves as a bank of sample questions, and the questions should be carefully selected based on the family or community member being interviewed. It is important to note that teachers need to be sensitive to the realities of their students, including those in foster care or those who do not have contact with family members.

Basic Questions

What is your full name, and why were you named this?

What are the names of your parents or guardians and siblings?

What is the date and place of your birth?

What was your schooling like? (That is, how did you get to school, what classes did you take, and what was your favorite subject?)

Family History Questions

Do you remember hearing your grandparents describe their lives? What did they say?

Do you remember your great-grandparents?

What do you know about them?

Who is the oldest person you can remember in your family from when you were a child?

What do you remember about that person?

What values were important for your family?

Lifetime Changes

What would you consider to be the most important inventions during your lifetime?

How is the world different now from when you were a child?

As you see it, what are the biggest problems that face our nation, and how do you think they could be solved?

Family Life

(NOTE: If your interviewee does not have children, then rephrase the next three questions to ask about nieces and nephews.)

Do you remember anything that your children did when they were small that really amazed you?

What is one of the most unusual things that one of your children did regularly when they were small?

What is the funniest thing that you can remember that one of your children said or did?

Where have you lived as an adult?

List the places and years that you lived there.

Why are you living where you are today?

Do you wish you lived somewhere else? If so, where?

Work

As a child, what did you want to be when you grew up?

What was your first job?

What kinds of jobs have you had?

How did you decide on your career?

If you served in the military, when and where did you serve, and what were your duties?

Personal

What person had the most positive influence on your life?

What did they do to influence you?

Is there a person who really changed the course of your life by something that they did? How did it happen?

Do you remember someone saying something to you that had a big impact on how you lived your life? Who said it, and what did that person say?

What was a struggle in your life that taught you an important lesson?

Source: Adapted from ReadWriteThink (2005).

Oral histories can also be driven by other links to the curriculum. Tapping into the knowledge of family or community members about social justice issues can sharpen students' knowledge of an event. For example, students need to learn about the role of protest and activism, so learning about a relative's memories of the Vietnam War era, the 1973 Wounded Knee Occupation, the 2018 March for Our Lives, the 2017 Women's March, or the protests fueled by George Floyd's killing are just a few examples of ways students can learn to connect history with their own community. As with a family oral history project, the class should generate interview questions so that they are tailored to the curricular purpose. Alternatively, these questions can be posed to a guest speaker invited to share their memories of the time being studied.

Empowerment Through Cultural Asset Mapping

Cultural asset mapping can be used as a springboard for empowering older students to shape the life of their community. This is especially important because empowered students can mobilize resources to achieve their goals. As well, empowered learners learn to see tasks as meaningful and impactful, recognize opportunities to exercise choice, and view themselves as competent to do so (Thomas & Velthouse, 1990).

> *Cultural asset mapping can be used as a springboard for empowering older students to shape the life of their community.*

The physical and cultural asset mapping of the community may expose barriers or gaps that challenge youth. For example, one community mapping project carried out by high school students exposed a lack of opportunities for positive youth development (Handy et al., 2011). Under educators' guidance as facilitators, students gathered data through interviews and focus groups conducted in the community. Then students worked with the superintendent, city leaders, and community organizers to create new programs for youth. Similarly, the children involved in the Alexander First Nation project made recommendations for community building improvements, including accessibility, and for the convenience store to offer more healthy food choices (DyckFehderau et al., 2013).

Let's look at another example of how asset mapping can work in the classroom and how it can benefit students. The Advancement Project is a public policy change organization rooted in civil rights activism (https://advancementproject.org). Like many such organizations, it uses asset mapping as a stepping stone to mobilize youth and adults to expand opportunities in communities and eliminate inequalities. The children involved in the Alexander First Nation project recommend facilitating discussion with the group that moves from identifying assets to identifying those missing. Use a similar process as the asset mapping outlined earlier in this chapter, but this time with a particular lens on a community issue. For example, the focus may be on access to affordable healthy food, books, positive youth development opportunities, or safe traffic passages for students walking to school. The identification of the issue should come from students, not from you.

Once students identify an issue, ask them to identify assets on a community map. Then lead them in a discussion of what they consider to be assets and nonassets for the problem they have identified. As a facilitator, keep your responses neutral. Don't make statements of agreement or disagreement. Instead, elicit responses from as many students as possible. Record their responses and conclusions so they can make decisions about next steps for taking action.

These next steps typically involve conducting interviews with other members of the community. The Advancement Project uses interviews to identify "ground truth data"—the lived experiences of people. As with other interviews, students can jointly compose questions to ask interviewees. In addition, they will need support in compiling their findings and developing a report. Students also benefit from a plan to share their findings with others. Teach students about ways to engage with local government and community organizations. These include actions such as writing letters, partnering with community nonprofits, presenting their results and recommendations to the city council and the school board, and posting on social media.

Pause and Ponder

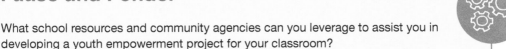

What school resources and community agencies can you leverage to assist you in developing a youth empowerment project for your classroom?

SCHOOL RESOURCES AND COMMUNITY AGENCIES	RESOURCES	CONTACT PERSON AND INFORMATION
School Clubs		
District Youth Empowerment Initiatives and Community Organizations Serving Youth		
Municipal Organizations Serving Youth		

Be a Strength Spotter

Asset mapping is a way to help students learn about themselves and the sources of strength they can draw upon. But this is also a way to learn more about our students so we can teach using a culturally relevant stance. As educators, we are surrounded by measures of student competence that reflect the dominant culture of schooling. As social justice educators, we must broaden our lens of children and the community to include strengths not typically appreciated or celebrated by the dominant culture in schools.

We use the term *strength spotter* quite intentionally. You've probably seen a spotter in a gym as an athlete works out with heavy weights. Being an effective spotter requires more than just standing nearby waiting for something bad to happen. The first requirement is that the spotter knows the athlete. A good spotter uses a "spot-on" approach, meaning they're actively engaged and ready for anything. A good spotter doesn't lift the weight for the athlete. Instead, they allow the athlete to work through the "sticky spot" when they are struggling a bit. That's how the athlete gets stronger. Katie Chasey (2013), a strength and conditioning coach, says that the spotter's stance is crucial, as the goal is to create "a larger base of stability." She goes on to say that if a lifter begins to fail, not just struggle, spotters should "never try to save the bar, just your lifter and yourself." As strength spotters in the classroom, isn't that what we do? We offer a large, stable base for our students and let them struggle a bit to get stronger, but support them if they fail. Knowing the assets our students bring to the classroom allows us to know our "athletes" and increase their strengths.

Pause and Ponder

The following comes from Kathryn Haydon at Sparkitivity. Take a look at the T-shirts in Figure 5.8. Which resonate most strongly with you? Which would you be proud to wear, because you feel they describe you? Choose as many as you'd like.

_____

_____

_____

_____

_____

_____

_____

Figure 5.8 Creative Personality Traits

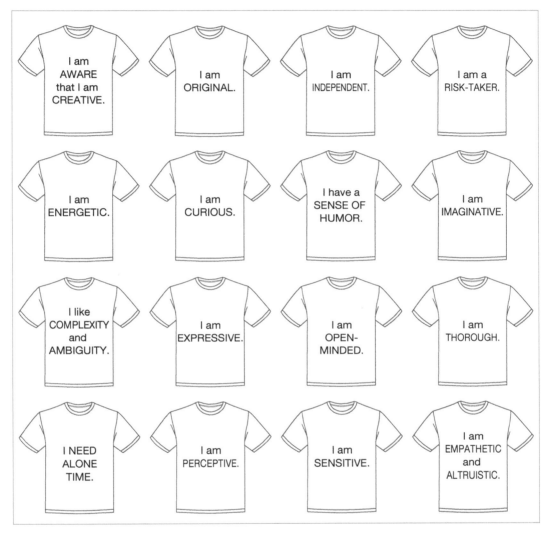

Source: Adapted from Sparkitivity, https://sparkitivity.com. T-shirt images courtesy of fongfong2/iStock.com.

You may have chosen them all, or you may have chosen a handful. Now look back on your T-shirts and pick your top three. Then pick your top one. Write your creative personality trait in a personal journal, on the whiteboard, or any place that serves as a reminder.

Use the same image (Figure 5.8) and pick T-shirts for your students. Begin with a student who challenges you—maybe one who has a reputation through the school. Did you find that difficult?

Now, turn your attention to Figure 5.9. Notice that these T-shirts have the same creative personality traits as Figure 5.8, but each trait is accompanied by the "counterfeit" version that negatively impacts our perception of students. So often the problems that students manifest in class result from these intense creative strengths that lack avenues for expression.

Intentionally work to view students through the personality traits that spot the strengths in students. Consider writing these creative personality traits next to student names on a class list.

Figure 5.9 Creative Personality Traits and Their Counterfeits

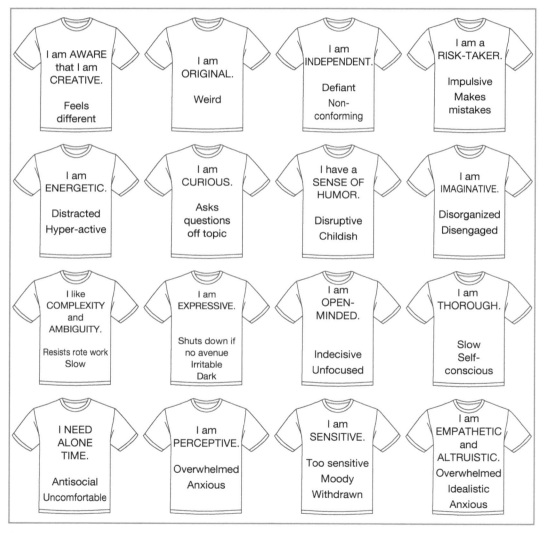

Source: Adapted from Sparkitivity, https://sparkitivity.com. T-shirt images courtesy of fongfong2/iStock.com.

Conclusion

Deficit thinking is harmful because it affects the expectations we hold for students. Asset mapping begins with recognizing the immense value in our students' identities, which adds to their ability to achieve great things—not despite their culture, but because of it. One way to support student empowerment is to start with interactively mapping the physical community that is connected to student lives. Then continue the work by mapping intangible cultural assets and involving family and community members to add dimension to understanding the richness of student cultures. As social justice educators and strength spotters, we empower these young activists to engage in their own social justice pursuits.

NOTES

3-2-1 Chapter Reflection

Now take an opportunity to think about the content of the chapter and what it means to you.

- What are three important ideas from this chapter?

_____

_____

_____

_____

_____

- What are two action steps you can take based on this chapter?

_____

_____

_____

_____

_____

- What is one idea or concept you would like to explore further?

_____

_____

_____

_____

_____

CHAPTER 6

Ethnic–Racial Identity Development

. . . .

> When those who have the power to name and to socially
> construct reality choose not to see you or hear you . . . when
> someone with the authority of a teacher, say, describes the
> world and you are not in it, there is a moment of psychic
> disequilibrium, as if you looked in the mirror and saw nothing.
>
> —Adrienne Rich

As educators, it is our professional responsibility to assist in students' ethnic and racial identity development, even if the goal is solely to support students' self-reflection. Students construct their identities through the experiences they have been exposed to. Therefore, social justice educators must encourage students to explore their ethnic and racial backgrounds. And honestly, we need to provide our white students with opportunities to understand that their identity development cannot be at the expense of others or be used to oppress others. We must offer all students opportunities to see themselves in the curriculum, hold conversations about social injustices, and explore their personal histories.

Let's see what this might look like at school, using a fictional teacher based on an actual classroom situation. It is the beginning of the school year, and Robert Tanielu, a middle school social sciences teacher, introduces the "all about me" activity to his students. The activity is designed for students to explore their personal experiences and dive deeper into their families' history and traditions. Mr. Tanielu is eager to learn valuable information about his students and their families through the presentations they will deliver to the class.

95

As he introduces the "my family history" portion of the project—a piece in which his students are tasked with interviewing a family member to discover more about their origin—he overhears a conversation from a Mexican American student who is sitting near his podium.

The student says, "Why do I care about where my family comes from? I mean, they're from there, I'm not, and I've never even been there."

Some educators in this position might think, *What does this mean? Is the student not interested in learning more about their ethnic history?* However, because Mr. Tanielu has had some prior experience with adolescents' ethnic and racial identity development, he understands that this student is exhibiting behavior associated with an unexamined ethnic identity (Phinney, 1989). Many times young people have not yet explored their ethnic identity or have little personal connection to it, which is crucial to their overall identity formation. Therefore, Mr. Tanielu understands that as a social justice educator, it is important for him to introduce his students to learning opportunities that allow them to explore their identities and see themselves in interactions with the world. By covering state standards in the curriculum that allow, or even welcome, students to explore ethnic and racial identity, Mr. Tanielu increases the likelihood his students can embark on a journey of developing a secure and stable understanding of self.

Ethnic–Racial Identity

The journey to be a social justice educator includes facing the daunting challenge of assisting our students in investigating their ethnic and racial identities. What is identity? According to renowned psychologist and theorist Erik Erikson, identity is derived from a series of internal challenges young people face throughout childhood and adolescence. Erikson (1968) described these developmental challenges as the identity crisis, "a crucial moment, when development must move one way or another, marshaling resources of growth, recovery, and further differentiation" (p. 16). Erikson believed that the methods young people use to resolve these crises and challenges result in shaping their identity and future development. With that in mind, if our students are shaping their identity during these developmental stages of their lives, why don't we consistently support their need to explore their ethnic and racial identities in school?

As social justice educators, we must strive to change the status quo.

One of the reasons may be due to a lack of emphasis on the topic in many teacher preparation programs (Branch, 2020). Yet a meta-analysis of forty-seven ethnic and racial identity studies found positive correlations to achievement for minoritized children and adolescents (Miller-Cotto & Byrnes, 2016). In addition, a teacher's implicit biases and stereotypes about ethnic and racial groups can significantly impact educators' expectations for the students in their classroom (Bell et al., 2007). Failing to address the ethnic identity development of our students perpetuates "eth-nically irrelevant teaching, teaching that assumes [w]hiteness as normative and ethnic groups as irrelevant" (Branch, 2020, p. 2). As social justice edu-cators, we must strive to change the status quo.

Developmental Stages of Ethnic Identity

Betancourt and López (1993) use the term *ethnicity* to reference a group characterized by a common nationality, culture, or language. Ethnic identity refers to a commitment to a cultural group and engagement in its cultural practices (Helms, 2007). For centuries, minoritized ethnic and racial groups have learned in a European American–centered curriculum. Consequently, there is an assumption that a dominant culture views other ethnicities as lesser (Phinney, 1989). Students internalize these negative views about themselves and other historically marginalized people.

When educators identify where students are in their ethnic iden-tity quest, it is beneficial to teaching and learning. Phinney's model (Figure 6.1) serves as a frame to understand where students are on the ethnic identity development continuum: unexamined ethnic identity, ethnic identity search/moratorium, and ethnic identity achievement.

Figure 6.1   Continuum of Ethnic Identity Development

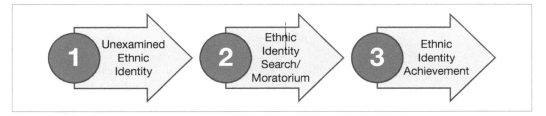

Stage 1: Unexamined Ethnic Identity: Students in this stage may have adopted the values and beliefs of the dominant culture but not explored their own ethnic identity. At this stage, students' unwillingness to explore their ethnicity can often lead them to adopt negative, prevailing views from a dominant culture about their ethnicity. Students at this stage have little experience in exploring their ethnicity and have little understanding of how minoritization of their ethnicity impacts them or others (Marcia, 1980).

Stage 2: Ethnic Identity Search/Moratorium: During the second stage of Phinney's model of ethnic identity formation, students have started to reflect on and explore their personal relationships with their ethnicity. This stage can be marked by an event that causes the students to explore their ethnic identity further. This stage is paramount in their ethnic identity development process. In this stage, students might be confused about their ethnic identity; however, they have decided they want to research, reflect, and learn more.

Stage 3: Ethnic Identity Achievement: The third and final stage represents the ideal outcome for students. Students feel proud and comfortable with who they are. They clearly understand their ethnicity, and they have come to accept the differences between their ethnicity and the dominant culture.

Multiracial Identities

Students are not unilaterally one ethnicity or race. The 2020 U.S. Census Bureau report (Jones et al., 2021) states that 10.2 percent of American adults identify as multiracial (up from 2.1 percent in 2013), but this is still likely an underestimate. The field of ethnic identity has broadened in this century. It is further informed by a more fluid ecological approach that recognizes that people may self-identify in more than one way. Instead of thinking of ethnic identity development as stages, think of it as patterns of identity that recognize the intersectionality of people's identities, and the influence of contexts that shift identities (Renn, 2008). Examine these identity patterns:

- A student holds a *monoracial identity* and chooses to identify with one of their heritage backgrounds.

- A student holds *multiple monoracial identities*, shifting according to the situation. Personal and contextual factors affect which of the student's heritage groups they identify with at a given time and place.

- A student holds a *multiracial identity*. They elect an identity that is neither one heritage nor another, but of a distinct "multiracial" group on par with other racial categories.

- A student holds an *extraracial identity* by deconstructing race or opting out of identification with U.S. racial categories. This pattern represents their resistance to what they may see as artificial categories that have been socially constructed by the dominant, monoracial, white majority.

- A student holds a *situational identity*, identifying differently in different contexts. This describes a fluid identity pattern in which the student's racial identity is stable, but different elements are more salient in some contexts than in others.

None of these identity patterns are inherently "right" or "wrong." However, suppose a student's adherence to a monoracial identity stems from limited knowledge about their cultural and ethnic influences or from negative self-concepts. In that case, the student is psychologically at risk. Studies show that adolescents who accurately represent their multiple heritages have higher self-esteem and self-efficacy, and they are less vulnerable to stereotype threat (Bracey et al., 2004; Shih et al., 2007).

Social justice educators can support students in their journey to investigate their ethnic and racial identities, especially students who have been historically marginalized and underserved. Educators validate who learners are by allowing students to learn about the richness of their culture, values, and traditions. Learners can explore their personal histories and deepen their sense of pride in their ethnic and racial identities. In turn, these students will be better prepared to counterargue biased and prejudiced opinions about them.

Pause and Ponder

Use the following needs assessment to identify where your school is positioned in terms of ethnic and racial identity practices. On a scale of 1 (*not a priority*) to 10 (*highest priority*), assess the extent to which the statements are a priority at your school. Then use the None/Some/Most/All range to estimate the consistency across the school campus.

STATEMENT	PRIORITY (1–10)
1. Texts used reflect the histories of students in the school and of those not represented among the student body.	
NONE (0%–10%) SOME (11%–50%) MOST (51%–89%) ALL (90%–100%)	
2. There are regular opportunities in classes to respectfully discuss ethnic and racial identities.	
NONE (0%–10%) SOME (11%–50%) MOST (51%–89%) ALL (90%–100%)	
3. Ethnicity-related questions are posed to students in the context of their learning to spark discussion.	
NONE (0%–10%) SOME (11%–50%) MOST (51%–89%) ALL (90%–100%)	
4. There are curricular opportunities to regularly profile historical and contemporary ethnic and racial identities (beyond specific months).	
NONE (0%–10%) SOME (11%–50%) MOST (51%–89%) ALL (90%–100%)	
5. Collaboration and cooperation are fostered among students in the classroom.	
NONE (0%–10%) SOME (11%–50%) MOST (51%–89%) ALL (90%–100%)	
6. Students explore their own identities in the context of their learning.	
NONE (0%–10%) SOME (11%–50%) MOST (51%–89%) ALL (90%–100%)	

Implementation

To increase the likelihood of learning and justice for all students, it's essential to provide opportunities for students to explore their ethnic and racial identities. Branch (2020) developed a model of ethnic identity exploration as a tool to organize the experiences students need in their schooling. Based on the existing ethnic and racial identity literature, Branch's model identified four themes that promote teaching strategies to foster knowledge of self and others. According to Branch, ethnic identity development should include the following dimensions:

1. Making connections with students' families about ethnicity and ethnic identity

2. Engaging students in ethnic identity discourse

3. Guiding students in the exploration of their ethnic histories, traditions, and customs

4. Introducing students to social justice role models within their ethnic groups

Furthermore, each idea encourages students to explore and gain a deeper understanding of their cultural backgrounds.

Make Connections With Students' Families About Ethnicity and Ethnic Identity

Our students' families and communities possess vast knowledge. Together they share a rich experience of culture, traditions, values, and history. As social justice educators who encourage students to explore their identities, we must seek to incorporate this knowledge into our classrooms. Schools should celebrate students' diversity and cultures.

Michael Girard, a high school history teacher, starts his classes every year with a "Where I'm From" poem frame (see Figure 6.2), inspired by George Ella Lyon's poem of the same name. (You can listen to the poet read her poem at www.georgeellalyon.com/audio/where.mp3.)

This activity allows Mr. Girard to further understand his students and the stories and experiences they share. The "Where I'm From" poem is an activity that is designed to make connections to families because it requires students to go home and hold conversations with family members to learn more about themselves. Then, by having the students share their stories with the class, Mr. Girard allows his students to learn about other cultures. In this way, he communicates that the ethnic backgrounds of his students and their families matter.

Figure 6.2 "Where I'm From" Poem Template

I am from _____ (specific ordinary item your family uses), from _____ (product name), and from _____ (another everyday item in your house).

I am from the _____ (description of your home, with an adjective and a sensory detail).

I am from the _____ (plant or other nature item) and the _____ (a different plant or other nature item).

I am from _____ (a family tradition) and _____ (a family tendency), from _____ (the name of an ancestor) and _____ (another ancestor) and _____ (your family name).

I am from the _____ (description of a family trait) and _____ (a family habit).

From _____ (something you were told frequently as a child) and _____ (another thing you were told frequently as a teen).

I am from _____ (representation of religion, or lack of it).

I'm from _____ (your place of birth and your family's heritages), and from _____ and _____ (two food items that are favorites of your family).

From the _____ (a family story about a specific person), the _____ (another detail about them), and the _____ (another story about a different family member).

I am from _____, _____ _____ (where your family keeps their pictures and mementos, and two more lines describing their worth and value).

online resources ⬆ Available for download at **resources.corwin.com/socialjusticeeducator**

Adriana Hernandez, a middle school English teacher, provides students with the opportunity to learn about their families as they share artifacts that represent their identity or the ethnic backgrounds of their families. These artifacts revolve around culture, values, traditions, nationality, and customs. This opportunity results in quite a range of artifacts, from cultural icons to community members who come to speak to the class. Some students share a traditional game, story, or dance. Others share a piece of writing from an author that represents the culture of their family. And still others rewrite a children's story with their cultural perspective.

Ms. Hernandez notes, "The information we learn about the students and their families during this project is paramount to establishing our classroom climate." The artifact project highlights many of the differences and similarities of the students' ethnic backgrounds. Most importantly, it communicates that all students' ethnic backgrounds are equally valued and respected in her classroom.

Melissa Duran, a second-grade teacher, starts the school year with her students by establishing strong communication with families. She notes, "I want to get to know my students—who they are, who their families are, and how I can best support their child's needs."

To begin, she sends out questionnaires for the families to fill out. Upon receiving the responses, Ms. Duran then selects narrative and informational texts her students will read throughout the year. One of her main goals is that each student's ethnic and racial identities are represented in contemporary and historical terms.

She explains, "It's another way to connect with families. Last year I had a student who has a Native American heritage. I didn't want to limit his knowledge to historical contexts. I asked his parents for text recommendations. That's how I added *The Good Luck Cat* [Harjo, 2000] and *Stolen Words* [Florence, 2017] to my classroom library."

These are just a few examples of how teachers have attempted to make a connection between the family's ethnic identity and the classroom. These teachers have created a safe learning environment that celebrates and encourages the exploration of students' diverse ethnic backgrounds. By implementing lessons that address each learner's ethnic identity development throughout units of instruction, we will ensure that our students are on the journey to becoming aware of and comfortable with who they are.

Pause and Ponder

Consider what you have been learning in this chapter about ethnic and racial identities. Why is family involvement, whether direct or indirect, so crucial?

_____

_____

_____

_____

_____

_____

_____

Discourse

As educators, we must provide students opportunities to discuss course content in class and connect it to their life experiences. Allowing students to explore topics such as systematic racism, oppression, social justice, and social inequalities in developmentally appropriate ways is vital. As we have noted in other chapters, teachers must take a neutral position while facilitating these discussions and allow students to formulate their own opinions. Doing so will allow students to openly discuss their thoughts, opinions, and feelings in a safe, respectful, productive class environment.

Discussions of this nature should vary in difficulty and should always be carefully constructed to ensure that the conversations remain age- and grade-level appropriate. Before engaging in topics that some students and families might consider controversial, it is essential to teach students how to share and critique opinions thoroughly and respectfully. Students must understand that these discussions have no room for personal attacks. Their claims should align with age- and grade-level-appropriate argumentative writing and speaking and listening curricular standards. By teaching students how to respectfully agree and disagree with others' viewpoints, schools prepare students to advocate for themselves and be critical consumers of information.

Mike Rossi, a high school social studies teacher, incorporates student discussions into his daily lessons. He explains, "It is important to allow our students to develop their voice. Introducing discourse into my classroom has increased motivation for students to co-construct understanding, and students often advocate for the topic of the discussion we are having."

One of the many ways Mr. Rossi provides students with an opportunity to discuss controversial issues is by implementing a Four Corners activity. The activity requires students to choose a position on the topic and defend their thinking throughout discourse. As the students share their thinking, they attempt to convince the other students to understand their perspective and consider changing opinions. Let's see what this looks like in practice.

On this occasion, Mr. Rossi offers his students the following statement: "NFL players should be required to stand for the national anthem." The students quickly start jotting down arguments that they believe justify their position. When prompted, the students stand up and go to their perspective corners: *agree*, *strongly agree*, *disagree*, and *strongly disagree*. There are a handful of students in each of the four corners. When queued, they proceed to present their arguments respectfully to the class. Mr. Rossi interjects, prompts further thinking, and asks clarifying questions as needed throughout the discussion.

This activity allows the students to discuss a controversial real-life event that is a topic nationally. The themes identified by the students through the conversation include protesting, nationalism, First Amendment rights, social inequalities, racism, and police brutality. As a social justice educator, Mr. Rossi does not shy away from introducing topics that address ethnicity and race. Instead, he encourages his students to share their ideas, opinions, and questions with the class. He is aware that his students need a safe environment to learn and discuss issues that affect their lives outside of school.

As social justice educators, we must allow our students to learn from discussing topics that affect their ethnic and racial identity. A high school government and economics teacher, Jennifer Simons accomplishes this goal by incorporating structured debates into her curriculum. Her students explore topics such as standardized testing, housing redlining, and voter suppression through debates. Through their research on social injustice, her students learn about the detrimental impact that these practices have on minoritized groups, and they identify the skills and strengths of those who fight for change.

> *As social justice educators, we must allow our students to learn from discussing topics that affect their ethnic and racial identity.*

Mrs. Simons explains, "The debates allow our students to engage in the research, learn about the status quo, and create evidence-based arguments that seek change. They learn to see both sides of an issue, which allows them to formulate their stand on a particular topic."

According to Mrs. Simons, the introduction of debates has transformed her students, who are now actively seeking to gain a deeper understanding of social issues. The implementation of debates has not only allowed her students to explore controversial topics; it has also encouraged them to seek a change of what they perceive to be unjust.

When the students in Francisco Santos's second-grade classroom get ready for "group talk," they know that they are going to have opportunities to hear different opinions and share their own. One week, to prepare for group talk, Mr. Santos asks them to read the story *Catching the Moon* (Hubbard, 2005). Then they discuss the tenacity and perseverance of the young baseball player in the story, who is facing gender discrimination.

Today Mr. Santos's class is reading *The Proudest Blue* (Muhammad, 2019), which is about the first day that a child is wearing a hijab. After analyzing the poetic descriptions that Faizah, the narrator, uses to describe her sister's hijab, Mr. Santos asks his students to think about why the sixth-grade boys make fun of Asiya's hijab.

After independent think time, a student named Lucas turns to his group and says, "I think those kids have never seen a hijab before."

Another student, Alondra, replies, "I agree with Lucas, and just because they haven't seen one doesn't mean they should laugh at her. That is not nice."

The discussion continues as Mr. Santos poses more questions to the group. They discuss if Asiya should have said something to the bullies, what the hijab means to Asiya and her family, and what the students would have done if they were a character in the story.

As Mr. Santos reflects on the discussion, he notes, "Empathy strengthens our classroom community. We are learning to understand the feelings of others and how to be respectful of cultural differences. But it is more than accepting differences; it's more about appreciating our differences."

Pause and Ponder

How are you providing students with an opportunity to discuss issues that are affecting minoritized ethnic and racial groups? What prompts can you use to facilitate these discussions?

_____

_____

_____

_____

_____

_____

_____

As social justice educators, we must continue seeking opportunities to develop our students' ethnic and racial identities. We can accomplish this goal by allowing students to explore their ethnic histories, values, traditions, and customs. Because our curriculum is centered on the European experience, many of our students do not learn about their own culture's history. So often, they have seen their ethnicity and racial groups represented as inferior. Social justice educators must attempt to combat this misrepresentation every day in their classrooms. By encouraging students to research their own ethnic and racial background, we can help ensure that learners have an opportunity to construct their ethnic and racial identity in a way that is based on well-rounded research.

Julio Vásquez, a fifth-grade teacher, approaches this objective by encouraging students to learn more about their ethnic and racial identity through a series of monthly engagement activities. Dr. Vásquez explains, "I wanted to encourage our students to learn about their ethnicity and race. However, I didn't want it to be one project that the students quickly forget about upon completion. Instead, I decided to split the exploratory, research portion of the project into a monthly task."

Dr. Vásquez believes that this project, in which students research their history one theme at a time, allows the conversation to be constant throughout the year: "We learn about celebrations, traditions, and historical events each month. Students gain an awareness of significant events of their peers' cultures that they would otherwise not gain not knowledge on."

At the end of the year, Dr. Vásquez has his students reflect upon the values, characteristics, and histories that they have learned about. He hopes that by exploring their ethnic and racial background, his students will further understand their ethnic and racial identities.

For students to reach the optimum stage of their ethnic identity, they must clearly know where they come from, their values, and their history. Social justice educators seek to implement these types of explorative projects in their curriculum to promote ways for students to learn about their ethnic and racial backgrounds.

Pause and Ponder

What projects, activities, and assignments do you implement in your classroom to encourage ethnic and racial identity exploration? What projects are you interested in bringing into your classroom?

_____

_____

_____

_____

_____

_____

_____

_____

Social Justice Role Model

When we think of social justice role models, renowned figures such as Martin Luther King Jr., Cesar Chavez, and Susan B. Anthony may quickly come to mind. Year after year, students in our educational system learn about their fight for social justice, their accomplishments, and their contributions to society. However, the truth is that students usually learn about these leaders in isolated units, or perhaps through an independent reading assignment, without being able to make a connection between their accomplishments and our students' life. More needs to be done to make these connections for our students.

For example, today, students might hear about Malala Yousafzai, an education activist who was shot while on the school bus because she advocated for girls' right to learn in Pakistan. Or they might turn on the television to see stories about public sports figures such as Colin Kaepernick, a former professional football player who protested against police brutality by kneeling during the national anthem. Or they may hear about Megan Rapinoe, a professional soccer player and a social activist who advocates for equal pay and LGBTQ+ rights. While these figures are fighting to keep social justice at the forefront of the political stage, our job as social justice educators is to connect these events to the issues that our students are facing in their communities.

> *Our job as social justice educators is to connect these events to the issues that our students are facing in their communities.*

With that in mind, historical and public figures might feel too distant for our students. In their eyes, these figures might be too far removed from their daily lives. Instead, we can introduce social justice leaders from the community to our students. This allows us to utilize the local leaders' vast knowledge, history, traditions, and values.

Imagine the impact that community leaders who represent our students' ethnic and racial backgrounds will have when they share their stories, experiences, and successes in dealing with the social injustices that our learners face in the same community. These experiences will be relevant to the students, who will identify with the community leaders and begin to understand that success is attainable.

As educators, we must make connections with our community so we can invite local leaders to hold these conversations with our students. For example, when Todd Gloria—the first person of color and the first openly gay person to be elected mayor of San Diego, California—visits high schools, students want to know how he overcame the bias in society to be elected. Other social justice leaders can also provide examples of challenges they have faced and hurdles they have overcome.

Readings That Represent

The readings that we assign students send a powerful message about importance. As Bishop (1990) noted, text selections should provide students with both mirror and window opportunities. Mirrors allow students to see themselves in the selected texts, and windows allow them to experience cultures that are different from their own. Bishop argued that both are important, yet many classrooms lack mirror text opportunities, and marginalized students mostly read about white people.

Tonia Soto, a third-grade teacher, says, "I'm pretty intentional about this. For the lessons I do with the whole class, I choose texts written by and about people of color three times for every white one. I know that there are great texts written by white authors about the white experience, and I want my students to know some of those stories. But, I want to flood them with texts that build their ethnic and racial identity." She explains, "I organize my class around themes. I select a book to read in class that helps students understand the theme, and then I create a choice book list so that students make choices. This way, I can balance having my students read about people who look like them and people who don't."

Middle school teacher Rosie Mulina notes that she creates short story book clubs so that students can talk with others about ethnic and racial identity. She says, "In my class, we are very explicit about ethnic and racial identity. I tell them about why I have selected the texts for the clubs, and then they meet with me about which ones they want to read."

She explains, "I talk with them about getting to know themselves and others. I have three questions posted behind me on our video meetings: *Who writes the stories? Who benefits from the stories? Who is missing from the stories?* These questions are the focus of our conversations as we talk about the short stories. I want to make sure that my students come to understand that stories are important and that they shape how we think, so we need to be careful about analyzing those questions."

Pause and Ponder

Think back to your own experience as a K–12 student. What were the opportunities in your school experience for investigating your ethnic and racial identities? What benefits could your students perceive from these opportunities? What are your worries or concerns about engaging in this type of work in your classroom? What resources do you have to collect and organize to support your efforts?

_____

_____

_____

_____

_____

_____

_____

_____

_____

Conclusion

As social justice educators, it is important to create opportunities for students to explore and understand their own ethnic and racial identities. To begin, we can work to understand the developmental stages of ethnic identity and the patterns of multiracial identities. We can also encourage family involvement to help bridge the gap of cultural knowledge that might exist between us and some of our students. Ultimately, we need to create a classroom culture that supports our students' ability to listen to other perspectives, generate their own opinions, respectfully disagree with each other, and use these discourse opportunities to shape their identity.

Powerful practices include making clear connections for students to see role models and activists from their community. The historical figures we choose to study, the perspectives of history that we highlight, and the diversity of heroes in stories we read and assign to learners all signal to students whether their ethnic and racial identities are valued in the classroom.

3-2-1 Chapter Reflection

Now take an opportunity to think about the content of the chapter and what it means to you.

- What are three important ideas from this chapter?

_____

_____

_____

_____

_____

- What are two action steps you can take based on this chapter?

_____

_____

_____

_____

_____

- What is one idea or concept you would like to explore further?

_____

_____

_____

_____

_____

CHAPTER

7

Family and Community Engagement

When you make the effort to speak someone else's language, even if it's just basic phrases here and there, you are saying to them, "I understand that you have a culture and identity that exists beyond me. I see you as a human being."

—Trevor Noah

Throughout this book, we have emphasized the importance of recognizing and honoring the multiple facets of each student's individual identity. In this chapter, we focus on the dynamics of our engagement as educators with students' most frequented and immediate surroundings and experiences outside of the classroom—their families, guardians, and communities. Through the lens of social justice, we must view all students as protagonists, each at the center of their own unique macrocosm comprised of prominent experiences, people, and places. Without placing blame, it is imperative to recognize that the depths of students' lives and relationships outside of school can easily escape teachers. The little time teachers truly have with students in the classroom only allows for a glimpse into their students' lives, especially when considering the many responsibilities teachers are accountable for on a day-to-day basis. Still, an awareness of how our students engage with their families and communities is of particularly great concern for those of us who teach in diverse communities. It is important for us to recognize and acknowledge that our students' home lives may represent a significant departure from our own childhood and our own participation in the dominant culture.

This is precisely where this chapter comes into play. Up to this point, in our own work toward becoming social justice educators, we have examined our understandings, behaviors, and practices and sought to reframe our orientation toward all students to recognize and alter patterns of inequity. This chapter invites you to take this practice one step further: to seek *the perspectives of students' family members and communities about the students' lives.* This task is integral to the work of social justice educators because it allows us to embrace an open mindset for engaging with families and communities, and it allows us to develop skills in building meaningful partnerships that benefit all stakeholders. When you include family and community voices in your classroom, you not only support students' achievement and growth; you also engage in a necessary part of our work as allies in the fight for equitable education.

Pause and Ponder

Think of a student with whom you have built a strong relationship. Who are the adults most prevalent in their life? What support system do they have outside of school? What ties do they have with the community outside of their home? Can you envision these webs of connections for any other students? What if you could build this type of relationship with all your students?

_____

_____

_____

_____

_____

_____

_____

_____

The Value in Family and Community Partnerships

Teachers occupy a fraction of space within each of their students' individual macrocosms (webs of social contexts), and their presence is filled with potential for inspiring profound learning and growth. Such potential is more readily realized when educators are well versed in the social contexts students navigate outside the classroom. A strong connection to students' families and communities provides teachers with access to multiple perspectives that inherently include the variation in students' lives in terms of family structures, values, attitudes, languages, communication patterns, and access to socioeconomic resources. The better teachers understand these perspectives, the more responsive their instruction is to the realities of students' lives.

Teachers find new pathways to empathy and connection when they adopt this more inclusive lens. For example, when educators develop a deep familiarity with their students' families and communities, they gain greater insight into the students' patterns and strengths, and they heighten their awareness and sensitivity toward their students' challenges. This approach also provides educators with a highly relevant frame of reference for engaging with students, which can be particularly useful when the lines of academic communication break down. Furthermore, teachers who make an effort to venture deeper into the real worlds of students acquire new levels of social-emotional expertise that enable them to bring a reassuring sense of comfort and home into the classroom.

Relationships between educators and students' families and communities—when established upon foundations of trust, communication, and authenticity—can ultimately produce a powerful new language and culture for teachers and students to share. Conversely, when the ways of life that are most familiar to students are nonexistent in the classroom, learners are forced to navigate two separate worlds that have no apparent connection. The more that connection eludes them, the less access they have to opportunities for meaningful participation in the academic environment. This phenomenon is unique to students from culturally and linguistically diverse backgrounds, and it warrants close examination and thoughtful action by social justice educators.

NOTES

Pause and Ponder

An underutilized dimension of social justice teaching is partnering with families and the community. Analyze your current status with families and use a scale from 1 (*weak*) to 5 (*strong*) to reflect on your practices and plan actions.

PRACTICE	STRENGTH (1–5)	ACTION STEPS
I have daily interactions with families.		
I have an understanding of families' aspirations for their children.		
I have regular two-way communication routines with families.		
Families contact me about concerns.		
Families contact me about celebrations.		

How might you strengthen your relationships with families?

_____

_____

_____

_____

Potential Barriers to Family and Community Involvement

Strong partnerships are made possible when teachers approach families and communities as entities of immense value. After all, a wholehearted belief in the value of an endeavor is a powerfully motivating factor in seeing it through, despite whatever challenges arise. This mindset is essential for teachers to embrace and project as they initiate relationships with families and communities, especially those families who have previously experienced barriers to engagement.

The families and communities that have historically been most involved in schools are those whose home cultures closely align with the behaviors, values, and social norms reflected in schools. Unsurprisingly, culturally and linguistically diverse and lower-income families are underrepresented in school-level decision making and opportunities for engagement (Brewster & Railsback, 2003). This disparity exists not because the families lack interest or willingness to get involved with their students' education but as a result of a difference in the needs, values, and levels of trust a family or community places in the educational system (Antunez, 2000; Goddard et al., 2001).

Productive interactions between families, communities, and educators may be hindered by barriers on either side of the relationship (Onikama et al., 1998). Regardless of where they originate, obstacles to engagement point to key areas of growth for improved communication and understanding. The table in the next Pause and Ponder feature outlines potential barriers from the perspectives of family, community members, and educators.

> *Obstacles to engagement point to key areas of growth for improved communication and understanding.*

NOTES

Pause and Ponder

Consider the following barriers and note the ways that they can be overcome.

PROBLEM SOLVING: FAMILY AND COMMUNITY ENGAGEMENT	
BARRIERS	**SOLUTIONS**
Language If little to no English is spoken at home, parents/guardians and families may feel uncomfortable when visiting the school. They might have difficulty expressing themselves and understanding what is being communicated.	
Life Obligations Family members might have multiple responsibilities inside and outside of the home. School meetings can conflict with their already busy day, forcing family members to choose between school events or meetings and their source of income or responsibilities.	
Views on the Family's Role in Education Some cultures view educators as authority figures who are not to be questioned. This cultural lens may steer family members away from making decisions about their student's education.	
Discomfort Lack of familiarity or comfort navigating the social context of schools may serve as a barrier to engagement.	

PROBLEM SOLVING: FAMILY AND COMMUNITY ENGAGEMENT	
BARRIERS	**SOLUTIONS**
Negative Experiences Previous negative interactions with schools and school personnel (condescension, refusal to help), whether as adults or as students themselves, might make it difficult for family members to view school as an approachable institution.	
Limiting Beliefs Limiting beliefs about families and communities (implicit bias that doesn't acknowledge the realities of all students) might hinder educators from partnering with families and communities.	
Condescension Condescension toward family members who are not familiar with any aspect of education, including grading, curriculum standards, attendance requirements, communication norms, and parent–teacher interactions, could cause family members to avoid interactions with the educator or the school.	
Training and Education Lack of training and education might make it difficult for educators to know how to engage the family and community. Teachers might struggle with knowing how to build relationships with families and communities. Teachers might not have training on how to identify strengths within families or communities or how to address adversity.	

Pursuing the active engagement of families and communities is not a small or an easy task, but these barriers must be addressed and resolved. When family engagement is not prioritized as an ongoing commitment, families remain excluded, miss opportunities to discover the value in their participation, and may come to view their involvement as unimportant (Weiss et al., 2009).

Trust

The engagement of families and community members depends heavily on strong, trusting relationships (Gorinski & Fraser, 2006). Trust is a key piece to the development of personal connections that serve as a bridge between the cultures within the home and at the school site and classroom.

> *The engagement of families and community members depends heavily on strong, trusting relationships.*

Trust can be defined as a "willingness to be vulnerable to another party based on the confidence that the latter party is benevolent, reliable, competent, honest, and open" (Hoy & Tschannen-Moran, 2003, p. 189). If we ask the families and communities to trust us as educators, then we must demonstrate that we are qualified, fair, and dependable—that we have their child's best interests at heart (Bryk & Schneider, 2002).

Trust is built over time, based on daily interactions, and it requires both sides to demonstrate consistent behaviors. Unfortunately, due to the variety of roles and responsibilities that most adults have, time is not on our side when developing trust. Instead, we tend to rely on the other person's reputation and on something we have in common: race, gender, age, religion, or upbringing (Bryk & Schneider, 2002). When there are fewer things in common between the families and communities and educators, the trust we seek will take more time to develop. Ultimately, when we build relational trust, we can demonstrate to students and families that their cultures are honored, celebrated, and included in the education we provide.

We each view the world through the unique lens of our culture: our systems of beliefs, customs, and behaviors shared by our experiences (Villegas & Lucas, 2002). Our jobs as educators provide a unique opportunity to interact with and participate in the growth and development of young people of diverse backgrounds.

By understanding the various cultural norms and beliefs within our schools, we can overcome the nuanced and sometimes challenging interactions between people of diverse backgrounds. Our students' success is improved when we understand and honor their unique cultures' attitudes, values, norms, and beliefs. In doing so, we communicate that we appreciate the students' unique cultures by more than the superficial act of acknowledging major holidays, dress, specific foods, and family customs. Honoring how culture might affect teaching and learning, social interactions between peers and adults, and cultural values positively impacts students' learning in the classroom.

Communication

Educators need to acknowledge that culture influences how people talk to one another—and that cultural differences can disrupt communication if they are not accounted for. A few important considerations include tone of voice, the amount of space between a speaker and listener, and eye contact. To be effective cross-cultural communicators, we must consider potential differences and aim to minimize the confusion and frustration that can arise when we engage with someone whose language, values, behaviors, and attitudes may differ from our own (Silver, 1997).

Effective cross-cultural communicators also do the following:

▷ Recognize that our culture may be reflected in different ways of communicating.

▷ Respect and accommodate cultural differences in communication.

▷ Apply strategies to deconstruct barriers to communication that arise from cultural differences.

Communication between schools and families must acknowledge and view diverse family cultures and values as strengths (Arias & Morillo-Campbell, 2008). When we ensure that our communicative practices are sensitive to the language and cultural backgrounds of our students' families and communities, we also support family and community engagement, because our communications allow our families and communities to participate in their child's education. Here are some steps we can take to improve our communications:

▷ Begin conversations on a personal level, and mix personal talk with academic talk during meetings and conferences.

▷ Utilize multiple communication methods, such as offering virtual meetings as well as emails.

▷ Listen and provide an opportunity for a two-way conversation.

▷ Meet families at the school site, home, or community location based on the choice that best serves the family.

▷ Express high expectations for communication between the family and the school.

▷ Invite families into the classroom to participate in the learning environment.

It is critical that educators understand that our cultural lens may differ from the cultural lenses of the families and communities that enroll in our schools. It is our duty as social justice educators and advocates to recognize the diverseness and honor the fact that those other cultural lenses are equally valuable to our own. When we take a step away from our personal lens and adopt a broader lens of our students' lives, we gain access to a variety of experiences, beliefs, and views. Let's look at an example.

The fourth graders in Alma Beltran's art rotation are working on their personalized flyers for their upcoming student-led conferences. The flyers include the date and time of the conference and a personalized drawing. The students are prepared with their portfolios to showcase their work and a reflection on their quarterly goals.

One of the fourth graders, Luis, proudly points to his drawing and says, "My flyer has a warrior on it, because my name means warrior. My mom and big brother are coming to my conference, and they are going to be so happy when they see all the work I've done."

Student-led conferences empower students to feel more in control of their own learning, and the personalized flyers are a welcoming invite to families to be a part of the conversation.

Pause and Ponder

What are ways that your school or your district communicates with families? In what ways do you receive information and input from families? How are families involved in decision making at both the school and district levels?

_____

_____

_____

_____

_____

_____

_____

It is important to remember that families and the community can be involved in many different types of ways. Look at Figure 7.1 and consider the list of different ways families and community members can be involved. Add to this list with ideas of your own.

Figure 7.1 Opportunities for Family and Community Involvement

- Volunteering to chaperone on field trips or events

- Creating school bulletin boards or displays

- Supporting a school club or a school sports team

- Assisting in classrooms

- Helping to welcome new families

- Helping from home (putting together packets, creating bulletin board or display items, etc.)

- Serving as an audience member at assemblies, sporting events, plays, and other events

- Reading to a class as a guest reader

- Preparing a talk for students on an interest or career

 Available for download at **resources.corwin.com/socialjusticeeducator**

Who Are Our Students' Families and Communities?

One of the first steps in engaging families and communities is developing an awareness of the demographic characteristics of our school or district. Educators are better suited to account for and accommodate the diverse needs of families when they have a clear picture of the students' backgrounds. While students must not be reduced to labels or stereotypes, demographic information can reveal a family's particular need for services like translation, food assistance, or tutoring. Figure 7.2 provides a starting point for collecting and looking at student demographics data to begin to understand the diversity of the families and communities we serve. By acknowledging and considering the unique economic status of our school's families, educators can better plan community and family engagement activities during times that are accessible for these families.

Figure 7.2 Demographic Data Questions

STUDENT DEMOGRAPHICS ACTIVITY	
STUDENT DEMOGRAPHICS DATA QUESTIONS	**OUR RESPONSE**
What demographic data are available at our school site? Can we use these data to further our understanding of the school's diverse families and communities?	
Do we have access to these data? If we do not, where can we obtain this information?	
What questions can we answer by using the demographic data found?	
What other data do we need that we don't currently have?	
What influence does this information have on our family and community engagement efforts?	

 Available for download at **resources.corwin.com/socialjusticeeducator**

For example, suppose the students' parents or guardians have more than one job. In that case, it may be difficult for them to attend meetings, volunteer in the classroom, or participate in other extracurricular activities typically found at the school site. Consider gathering information from families to understand how to best contact them and gain insight on what makes them feel connected to their school. Figure 7.3 provides some examples of questions that could be asked to understand family involvement from the perspective of the family.

Figure 7.3 Potential Survey Questions for Families

1.	What is the best way for us to contact you (phone call, email, mail, app, etc.)?
2.	When is the best time to reach you?
3.	What would make the classroom a comfortable and inviting place for you and your child?
4.	What makes you feel connected to your child's school?
5.	How well do the activities offered at your child's school match their interests?
6.	What else would you like us to know?
7.	How would you like to be involved? Here is a list of current opportunities.

 Available for download at **resources.corwin.com/socialjusticeeducator**

The connections we make with the communities we serve also bolster the relationships we strive for with families and students. For example, one elementary school, located adjacent to a large warehouse store, receives complimentary backpacks and school supplies from the store every year. The business also provides pumpkin pies for the school's annual Turkey Trot. The employees from the store often visit the school and cheer students on during their school events. By connecting with community businesses, educators can build relationships with institutions that can employ school graduates, sponsor events, offer scholarships, and build trade pathways.

To show the respect and competency that is needed for us to work with different cultures, we should seek opportunities to implement activities that bring us into our diverse populations' homes and community centers. This approach builds trust between the family and community systems and the school system. This is important to the success and achievement of our students, but it might feel like a daunting task at first. Consider taking an inventory of your school's or district's present practices that serve as a bridge between the school and community. Figure 7.4 provides ideas that can help focus our efforts.

Figure 7.4 Inventory of Present Practices of School, Family, and Community Partnerships

	VERY WELL IMPLEMENTED	GOOD START	NEEDS IMPROVEMENT	NOTES
We sponsor education workshops and other courses of training for parents and guardians.				
We ask families for information about children's goals, strengths, and talents.				
We sponsor home-visiting programs.				
We have formal conferences with parents and guardians at least once a year.				
We provide language translators or interpreters as needed.				
Staff members send home positive messages about students on a regular basis.				
We contact families of students having academic or behavior problems.				
We conduct annual surveys to identify interests, talents, and availability of volunteers.				
We have a family room for volunteer work, meetings, and resources for families.				
We schedule plays, concerts, games, and other events at different times of the day or evening so that all parents or guardians can attend some activities.				
We provide ways for families to be involved at home or in the community if they cannot volunteer at school.				
We conduct family nights or other workshops to help parents and guardians understand school subjects and learn ways to help their children at home.				
We have family representation on our School Council, School Improvement Team, or other school committees.				
We use email and quick surveys to obtain families' input and ideas on school policies.				
We work with local businesses, industries, and community organizations to put on programs and events to enhance student skills.				
We organize service *to the* community by students, families, and schools.				

Source: Adapted from Epstein, J. L. (2019).

 Available for download at **resources.corwin.com/socialjusticeeducator**

Conclusion

Inviting the voices of the other adults in our students' lives requires an open mind and heart. It may help us to think of our own lens as fluid rather than fixed. As individuals, our unique perspective on the world informs the attitudes, beliefs, and values we hold close to our heart. It is natural to want to share those with others, but as teachers who prioritize social justice, we have to parse out the personal from the professional, including all of the ostensibly basic assumptions and "should" statements we use to operate our lives. In doing so, we make space within ourselves to recognize, listen to, understand, and respond effectively to the identities, opinions, and experiences that differ from our own. Making that space takes work, but the reward for embracing this approach is a new lens primed for building relationships with families and communities.

NOTES

3-2-1 Chapter Reflection

Now take an opportunity to think about the content of the chapter and what it means to you.

- What are three important ideas from this chapter?

  _____

  _____

  _____

  _____

  _____

- What are two action steps you can take based on this chapter?

  _____

  _____

  _____

  _____

  _____

- What is one idea or concept you would like to explore further?

  _____

  _____

  _____

  _____

  _____

Racial Battle Fatigue in Schools

An African proverb says, "If you want to go fast, go alone. If you want to go far, go together."

It is difficult to underestimate the impact of fatigue on well-being and overall wellness. Fatigue, which is a symptom of other things, is often described as tiredness. Fatigue results from lifestyle choices, social experiences, psychological wellness, and overall well-being. It takes energy to process feedback from our daily interactions with people. Those experiences, and their processing, either give energy or drain it. There are also medical causes of fatigue, but this chapter focuses on how the situations and interactions people deal with daily in their workplaces, homes, and cities sometimes create race-related stress responses, which can take great amounts of mental and emotional energy to reconcile. This chapter explores how repeated exposure to racism and racial aggression negatively affects students, educators, and families.

Throughout this book, we've discussed the concepts of the dominant culture in a school and how members of that dominant culture belong to an intersectionality of groups. One of those groups is a racial group with which they identify to some degree. We have also discussed how social justice educators must remain aware that policies schools implement should not marginalize any groups.

Decision makers in dominant groups might fear people outside of their group to the point they create policies, unknowingly sometimes, that suffocate students' expression of their cultural identities. This suffocation of cultural self-expression sometimes prompts decision makers in dominant groups to suppress curricular activities that celebrate diverse cultures. These celebratory activities assist diverse students with self-actualization. As stated earlier, when decision makers fear the advancement of others, they (sometimes unconsciously) respond viscerally to actions they perceive could lead to other groups' advancement or expressions of self-pride.

When decision makers from dominant racial groups use their influence to derail other groups' advancement, they support the foundation of institutionalized racism in whatever sphere those decisions are being made. This may be why

- So few Black and Latino/a students can access advanced school courses

- Students of color are disproportionately suspended and expelled

- A low, disproportionate number of high-achieving students of color are awarded scholarships to attend college

- There are so few chief executives of color at Fortune 500 companies or in the nonprofit sector, let alone schools

While racial battle fatigue can afflict any person of color (e.g., Call-Cummings & Martinez, 2017), it tends to afflict Black people disproportionately (Smith et al., 2011). In schools, decisions that support institutionalized racism create an unwelcoming and stressful environment for students and families of color, particularly Black students and their families. As well, staff members of color, particularly Black staff members, disproportionately feel the weight of these decisions or feel walled-off from opportunities.

Decision making that affirms racial isolation and insensitivity creates a tone and temperament that saturates educational organizations and how people think of and treat students and staff of color. Over time, this tone and temperament can become institutionalized and define the culture of our schools. The harmful culture then becomes omnipresent and seemingly invisible; it may be viewed as "the way things are." Battling against this omnipresent, racially unfriendly sentiment day after day, month after month, year after year is exhausting. This led William A. Smith to coin the term *racial battle fatigue*.

Racial Battle Fatigue Defined

Racial battle fatigue is a "systemic race-related (racism-related) repetitive stress injury" (Lomotey & Smith, 2023, p. 143). It is the cumulative result of prolonged exposure to distressing mental and emotional conditions in a chronically unsafe or hostile environment. Racial battle fatigue is an interdisciplinary framework that considers the increased levels of psychological stressors and the resulting psychological, physiological, and behavioral responses associated with fighting racial microaggressions in mundane extreme environmental stress. Research shows that as Black Americans attain higher levels of education, they tend to experience higher levels of extreme environmental stress stemming from racial microaggressions.

To be clear, societal problems largely influence mundane extreme environmental stress across all education levels. For Black college graduates, racial microaggressions and societal problems contribute to approximately 40 percent of the mundane stress that Black Americans of this stratum experience (Smith et al., 2011).

Smith and colleagues (2011, p. 67) anchor some of their thinking about racial battle fatigue in Pierce's ideas (Pierce et al., 1978), including microaggressions, and suggest when examining "the substance of today's racism one must not look for the gross and obvious." Rather, we must identify and measure the impact of what Pierce called the "subtle, cumulative miniassault" of racial microaggressions (Smith et al., 2011, p. 67). This is an important idea, as it refocuses our attention from obvious, blatantly disrespectful behavior to subtle—but just as harmful—behaviors. These miniassaults are hurtful and have a cumulative impact on the mental health, physical health, and overall well-being of our students and their families, as well as our colleagues.

A news story titled "Discrimination Creates Racial Battle Fatigue for African-Americans" (Penn State, 2017) ran in a regional newspaper. The story reported on a press release documenting a research study led by psychology professor Jose Soto, who examined data from the National Survey of American Life, which surveyed 5,899 American adults. In the National Survey of American Life, the data set collected information on mental health and discrimination from 3,570 participants. In their analysis of the National Survey of American Life, Soto and colleagues found that

- 40 percent of the African Americans surveyed said they experienced some level of racial discrimination

- 4.5 percent of those surveyed said they suffered from general anxiety disorder

- Roughly 39 percent of Afro-Caribbeans surveyed reported they experienced some form of racial discrimination

- 2.69 percent of Afro-Caribbeans surveyed said they had developed generalized anxiety disorder

The researchers confidently concluded there was a connection between racism and severe anxiety and its impact on healthy functioning.

Racial battle fatigue is insidious. As educators, it's important for us to recognize racial battle fatigue because it is a hard thing to cope with; the sheer need to deal with it can add stress to the lives of our students, their families, and our colleagues. Here are some of the emotional and behavioral ways that the difficulty of coping with racial aggression and the stress racial aggressions cause may present at home or at school:

> Loss of appetite

> Overeating

> Smoking

> Consuming alcohol

> Self-isolating

> Performing poorly at school or work

Psychological responses to racial aggression and the stress of racial aggressions include the following:

> Anger

> Disappointment

> Worry

> Disbelief

There are also many physiological responses to racial battle fatigue. These may include

> Insomnia

> Chest pains

> Chronic headaches

> Shortness of breath

Black Americans also suffer from high blood pressure at higher rates than other groups (American Heart Association, 2022); it can be argued that a major contributing factor to this dangerous medical condition is their increased exposure to race-based hostilities.

NOTES

Pause and Ponder

Think about your work environment. Is your school or office a sanctuary that is free of racial battle fatigue? Is your workplace an area where people of color don't feel they need to deflect racism, stereotypes, and discrimination most days? Even schools comprised primarily of people of color can still experience racial battle fatigue if a school district superintendent or their supervisory proxies subject the school's leaders or teachers to race-based discriminatory attacks.

Social justice educators must be mindful of racial battle fatigue as they ensure that schools are safe and respectful learning environments for all students and staff members. Here is a list of some of the types of data we can examine to provide insight into not only our school's climate but also how racial battle fatigue may impact educators from marginalized groups in our workforce.

- **Staff attendance patterns.** Do the data provide any insight into how staff members may be experiencing the racial climate of a school?

- **The hiring practices of your school or district.** Do people of color apply to work at your school? If they apply, do they get hired at rates proportional to other groups? If they get hired, how long do they stay at the school?

According to the RAND Corporation report titled "Job-Related Stress Threatens the Teacher Supply," Black American teachers were twice as likely to leave the teaching profession than white teachers at the end of the 2020–2021 school year (Steiner & Woo, 2021). In *Time* magazine's reporting about Black American teachers leaving the profession, a teacher who formed an antiracism group for teachers who were contemplating quitting teaching summed up many Black American teachers' frustrations: "I was tired of being quiet . . . I was tired of sitting back so that [w]hite people could feel comfortable" (Carr, 2022).

As social justice educators, we need to understand that racial battle fatigue exists, and we need to behave in ways that hedge against how racial battle fatigue undermines the teaching workforce. We must refuse to be indifferent to racial battle fatigue, which negatively impacts our schools' ability to provide students with a diverse, high-quality teaching workforce.

Racial Battle Fatigue in Classrooms and Schools

It is fair to see schools and classrooms as the ultimate meritocracy. After all, schools are places where 1 plus 1 should always equal 2. Learners who answer ten out of ten questions correctly on a quiz should earn a perfect score and be regarded as masters of the content assessed on that quiz. Students on the team that crosses the finish line first in a relay race should be declared the winners. Schools are places where people can be judged for what they know, what they accomplish, and how they demonstrate academic and socioemotional competence.

Of course, in reality this is not always the case. Some leaders and educators in positions of influence perpetuate a workplace culture that heaps race-based stress into the lives of students and teachers. This manifests when students and teachers from marginalized groups are watched and policed by peers and adults for mundane, ridiculous reasons, while those who aren't people of color enjoy trust and freedom and aren't subject to heightened scrutiny. Another example is when employees and students of color feel so unwelcome on campus that they are compelled to carve out safe clubs and spaces for people of color—and even those "safe spaces" often become the subject of ridicule and attack.

Students engage more when they are learning in accepting and affirming environments. Unfortunately, some schools, let alone school districts, aren't accepting, affirming places for people of color. Instead, they are proverbial battlefields of race-based oppression purported as happy places. In reality, these battlefields of race-based oppression often engage in harmful acts like the following:

▷ Imploring their inhabitants of color to learn to cope with omnipresent feelings of racial oppression and the racial battle fatigue it causes them

▷ Suggesting visibly or invisibly that Black people are never quite "good enough" to earn promotions in the eyes of white peers and supervisors

▷ Treating communities of color in negative ways

▶ Disciplining Black students more harshly for the same offenses as white students (who may only be given a warning if they are disciplined at all)

▶ Forming predominantly white athletic teams with coaches who hurl racial slurs toward visiting athletes or their own

As an example, Sarah, who played basketball in high school, remembers that during one game, the opposing team threw tortillas on the court because Sarah's team was mainly Latina. What makes these schools or districts battlefields of race-based oppression is that consequences are rarely, if ever, given to the offending coach, team, principal, or school board members because nobody seems to think that behavior is problematic. This perpetuates the cycle by reinforcing the negative behavior, and it serves as a source of stress for minoritized students in schools, which causes fatigue.

Pause and Ponder

How can your school ensure that students of color are not receiving harsher consequences than their white peers?

_____

_____

_____

_____

_____

_____

_____

Students who go to faculty and staff for help from race-based attacks sometimes don't get help. In fact, the culture of race-based oppression is so firmly established in many schools and districts that students don't expect to be helped, so they don't even bother asking the adults in their schools for help. In some schools and districts, the battle theater of race-based oppression for students and staff of color is normalized and well established, and racial battle fatigue hangs in the air like misting rain. To students and staff, this omnipresent unfairness can appear to be impossible to wipe away or escape.

Alleviating Race-Based Oppression and Racial Battle Fatigue

As social justice educators, our attitudes, dispositions, and actions can help create positive conditions in schools and school districts that eliminate race-based oppressive battlefields and alleviate racial battle fatigue. While our actions may seem small, even imperceptible, they can have a tremendous impact on ensuring all students receive a high-quality education and a diverse workforce of educators in the aggregate. Figure 8.1 introduces an evaluation tool that prompts reflection on equity practices in school and can serve as a starting point for discussion. Lower scores indicate that the respondent feels less confident that their school environment values diversity. Higher scores indicate that the respondent feels more confident that their school environment values diversity.

As referenced in the survey, schools can help to alleviate the effects of racial battle fatigue when we create safe places for students to discuss culture, race, and identities. We can support safe places for students to think critically and be exposed to a wide variety of thinking. Students can have grade-level-appropriate conversations that align with learning standards.

Here are a few classroom examples in which teachers are creating opportunities for diverse thinking and discourse, but we know that there are a lot more possibilities.

> ▶ Middle school student Farida Bhat makes the observation that the censored books being discussed are mostly written by Latino/a, Black, and LGBTQ+ authors.

> ▶ After reading *The Girl Who Thought in Pictures: The Story of Dr. Temple Grandin* (Mosca, 2017), third-grader Jessica Thompson tells her book club group, "I think everyone has things that are easy for them and things that are hard for them too. I mean like Temple, her brain was great at making pictures and she could make farm inventions that other people couldn't make."

> ▶ In Charlie Scott's ninth-grade class, the students are seated for a "fishbowl" class conversation. Jenna occupies the empty chair to enter the conversation and says, "But it shouldn't just be us that are fighting sexual harassment at school. We need the guys to fight with us. We need them to know first how it affects us, then we need them to care enough to do something about it with us."

> ▶ High school senior and aspiring teacher David Perez prepares to give a presentation to his class discussing the school-to-prison pipeline and the percentage of incarcerated adults who read below a fourth-grade level.

> ▶ Kindergarten teacher Michaela Chen brings in a Filipino female firefighter for their unit on important community members.

Figure 8.1 Equity in School Reflection Tool

EQUITY IN SCHOOL REFLECTION TOOL (SHORT VERSION)				
	STRONGLY DISAGREE	DISAGREE	AGREE	STRONGLY AGREE
My school hires diverse faculty and staff.	1	2	3	4
Reflection				
My school retains diverse faculty and staff.	1	2	3	4
Reflection				
Racially/ethnically diverse students are suspended or expelled at rates proportional to their enrollment at my school.	1	2	3	4
Reflection				
I feel safe participating in discussions about educating students of color.	1	2	3	4
Reflection				
I have authentic relationships with staff outside my racial/ethnic group.	1	2	3	4
Reflection				
My school or district promotes diverse cultural expression.	1	2	3	4
Reflection				
Students in my school have told me they feel welcome at my school.	1	2	3	4
Reflection				
My school responds appropriately to incidents of harassment and discrimination.	1	2	3	4
Reflection				
Diverse perspectives are valued in my school.	1	2	3	4
Reflection				
I can be my authentic self in my school.	1	2	3	4
Reflection				
TOTAL				
OVERALL TOTAL SCORE				

Available for download at **resources.corwin.com/socialjusticeeducator**

Pause and Ponder

Which of the preceding examples resonate with you? What other ideas do you have for providing students with safe places to discuss race and identities?

_____

_____

_____

_____

_____

_____

_____

_____

Alleviating race-based oppression in school settings necessitates collaboration between site-based faculty, staff, and leaders; district-level leadership; and boards of education. Conditions to alleviate race-based oppression and resulting racial battle fatigue in schools can be created without the support of leaders outside of school sites; however, this is exceedingly difficult to accomplish. District and school board leaders tremendously influence working environments that create conditions for schools' success.

School boards and district superintendents can set policy that commits districts to antiracist behavior and drives equity-centered action steps in school staffing, funding, climate, and reporting of incidents that occur (Jones, 2020). They can also institute accountability mechanisms to ensure antiracist behavior and equity-centered action. School district superintendents can commit their districts to partnerships with equity-centered organizations and increase their districts' likelihood of sustaining commitments to antiracist behavior. Figure 8.2 addresses different categories for policies and what should be addressed within each category. For example, a policy around school environment should address the importance of an equity-oriented climate.

When district and school leaders set policies that commit schools to antiracist behavior and equity-centered action, it makes it easier for school-based staff to behave in antiracist ways, including addressing racist behavior when it arises and discussing race and inclusion whenever circumstances necessitate these conversations. It makes sense to teach faculty and staff how to support students and each other if an issue of race-based oppression or inequity arises in districts that have committed

Figure 8.2   Implementing Antiracist Policies in Schools

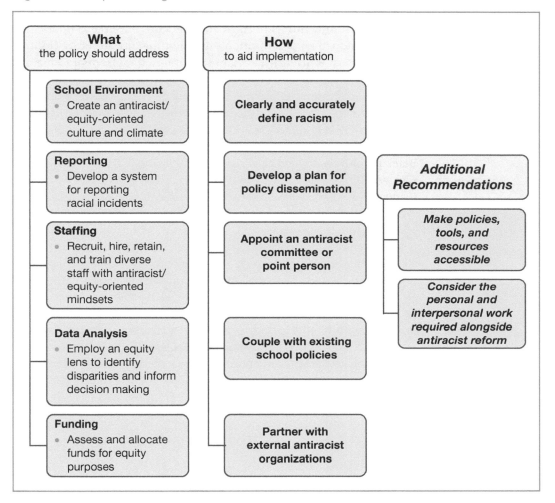

Source: Jones (2020).

to equity-centered action, diversity, and antiracist behavior. It also makes sense to teach how to ensure all students have equal access to curricular and extracurricular opportunities in districts committed to equity-centered action, diversity, and antiracist behavior.

Every school district has not committed to equity-centered action, diversity, and antiracist behavior—or at least that commitment has not crystallized into a board-approved policy. Still, these districts' students, families, and staff deserve to learn and work in safe and respectful learning environments. The needs and humanity of faculty, staff, and students of color in these districts matter. They deserve to feel safe and respected regardless of whether equity-centered action has been codified into board policy. It is up to social justice educators to ensure their work in schools helps all students receive free and appropriate education and that no person suffers race-based oppression in schools or the racial battle fatigue that often ensues.

While social justice educators are crucial to maintaining safe and respectful learning environments for all students and staff, it is notable that the most influential efforts to address workplace racial oppression start at the top of an organization's decision-making structure (Morris, 2020). To most efficiently alleviate school-based racial oppression and any resulting school-influenced racial battle fatigue, principals, central office administrators, and school board members must take up the mantle of learning and justice for all. In her *Forbes* article "How to Dismantle Racism in the Workplace: It Starts at the Top," Carmen Morris (2020) writes, "I have written previously about the dangers of hastily co-opting Black employees to lead the race equality agenda. The top dressing of race equality issues only serves to protract and exacerbate workplace inequalities. Many leadership teams remain content with procuring the services of their Black employees in an effort to make this change a reality."

We couldn't agree more.

This conundrum is a "Yes, and" situation and solution. *Yes*, all social justice educators must do what they can within their classrooms, offices, and related spheres of influence to address school-based racial oppression that results in racial battle fatigue. *And* leaders in an organization must make decisions in boardrooms, offices, and other spheres of influence—up to and including through institutional policymaking—not only to root out inequities that surface, but also to create workplace environments where racially oppressive behavior cannot take root. Racism is built and maintained with the muscle of institutional power. Dismantling it—at least, doing so efficiently—will benefit from this same muscle.

Navigating Racial Battle Fatigue and Race-Based Oppression

Understanding how unconscious racial bias relates to race-based oppression in schools helps social justice educators improve the educational experience of diverse groups of students. While it can be difficult, social justice educators must find the courage to hold their colleagues accountable when they do or say racially insensitive things. Admittedly, this is not always easy. Confronting inappropriate speech—let alone inappropriate action—can be uncomfortable. Still, this is an important way social justice educators can help dismantle racially oppressive educational environments.

Social justice educators must also be conscious of their own speech. They must guard against reinforcing race-based oppression in schools by using microaggressive, stereotypical, or racially insensitive comments toward others, regardless of whether the use is intentional or not. Social justice educators must not treat others like they are "less than" because of their race, gender, sexual orientation, or other manifestation of diversity or uniqueness. Social justice educators must not engage in microinsults: making comments toward others that are unintentionally discriminatory or belittle what makes others diverse. Finally, social justice educators can refrain from and confront microinvalidations: comments that invalidate or undermine the experiences of a marginalized group.

Healing Through Connections

The American Psychological Association (2021) advises those affected by racial trauma to share their difficult feelings with others to cope with the emotional, physical, and spiritual toll. It is prudent for justice-conscious schools and districts to create safe spaces for students and staff affected by racial oppression to process emotional difficulties they may be experiencing, especially if the district suspects students and staff workplace experiences may contribute to or exacerbate existing race-related stress.

Race-based affinity and employee resource groups are common. The Society for Human Resource Management (Taylor, 2019) provides guidance that is appropriate for adults and students. Affinity groups, just like school-based clubs and organizations, should be managed in alignment with anti-discrimination laws, such as Title VII of the Civil Rights Act of 1964, which prohibits discrimination based on sex, race, religion, and national origin (Taylor, 2019). Social justice–conscious schools and districts understand that being seen and heard is essential to coping with racial trauma. Social justice–conscious schools and districts will do what they can to create safe spaces for discussion, dialog, and connection among school and district community members who seek to heal from race-based oppression and the racial battle fatigue race-based oppression causes.

Jackson, a seventh-grade student at McKinney Middle School, notes, "I'm a friendly guy. I have friends from my classes, and I love to do neighborhood projects with my friends in the Students in the Community Club. But I feel like I can really be myself in our Black Student Union. Each group that I am a part of is important to me in different ways."

NOTES

_____

_____

_____

_____

_____

_____

_____

_____

_____

_____

_____

Pause and Ponder

What safe places and groups are available to your students to be able to share their feelings and receive support for traumas?

_____

_____

_____

_____

_____

_____

_____

_____

Conclusion

Racial battle fatigue, which has many harmful emotional, psychological, and physical effects, is caused by the stress of repeated exposure to racism. It can be alleviated when school boards and superintendents make a public statement expressing a commitment to antiracism, set policies to eliminate hiring and promotion disparities, and then actively promote a positive school culture for all students to thrive. Schools can alleviate racial battle fatigue for students by evaluating current practices and procedures for systemic racism, unintentional bias, unequal opportunities, and barriers to academic achievement for all learners. Further, as social justice educators, we can mitigate the trauma of racial battle fatigue by cultivating student voice and providing a safe place for difficult feelings to be expressed. A welcoming and inclusive environment will benefit the entire school community.

NOTES

_____

_____

_____

_____

_____

3-2-1 Chapter Reflection

Now take an opportunity to think about the content of the chapter and what it means to you.

- What are three important ideas from this chapter?

  _____

  _____

  _____

  _____

  _____

- What are two action steps you can take based on this chapter?

  _____

  _____

  _____

  _____

  _____

- What is one idea or concept you would like to explore further?

  _____

  _____

  _____

  _____

  _____

Conclusion

Sor Juana Inés de la Cruz, a Mexican writer and philosopher in the 17th century who was considered a rebel for wanting to obtain a formal education and for challenging the patriarchal society that she lived in, said, "No studio para saber más, sino para ignorar menos," which, translated, says, "I don't study to know more, but to ignore less." It is our hope that we learn and gain understanding together so that we have the skills to create learning environments for all our students that allow them to feel valued, respected, and successful.

As we wrote and discussed ideas for this book, it is important to note that we did not always agree with each other. Isn't that beautiful? The back-and-forth that goes into discourse helped each one of us grow and reflect. We are each still on a journey of our own understanding. We are social justice educators, not because we know all of the answers, but because our hearts and minds are open to understanding the barriers to and solutions for an equitable education for all students.

We understand that first we need to spend the time intentionally getting to know ourselves and understanding the impact of our experiences on our perspectives and worldview. We acknowledge that we all hold implicit biases, these patterns and shortcuts we have created in our minds. We acknowledge that they affect our thoughts, our words, and ultimately opportunities for our students. We can be more self-aware and honest with ourselves in confronting our implicit biases so that we can take action to reduce them. We also encourage readers to help students explore and develop their own ethnic and racial identities so they can see their identity as a source of strength. Racial battle fatigue, stereotype threat, and microaggressions are all barriers that are real and detrimental to students and educators, but the resources of our families, our communities, and our humanity will overcome these obstacles to a just education.

Paraphrasing Nezahualcóyotl, a 15th century poet and warrior, we love the beauty of nature, the songs of the mockingbird, the color of jade, and the perfume of flowers, but we love humankind the most. And we believe that the solution to the barriers discussed lies in the courage and vulnerability in all of us. We are thankful that you are on this journey with us.

References

Aboud, F. E. (1988). *Children and prejudice.* Oxford Basil Blackwell.

Agar, M. (2006). Culture: Can you take it anywhere? Invited lecture presented at the Gevirtz Graduate School of Education, University of California at Santa Barbara. *International Journal of Qualitative Methods, 5*(2), 1–12.

Allport, G. (1954). *The nature of prejudice.* Addison-Wesley.

American Heart Association. (2022, March 4). *High blood pressure among Black people.* https://www.heart.org/en/health-topics/high-blood-pressure/why-high-blood-pressure-is-a-silent-killer/high-blood-pressure-and-african-americans

American Psychological Association. (2021, June 11). *Managing your distress in the aftermath of racial trauma and stress.* www.apa.org/topics/racism-bias-discrimination/managing-distress-racial-trauma

Antunez, B. (2000). When everyone is involved: Parents and communities in school reform. In B. Antunez, P. A. DiCerbo, & K. Menken (Eds.), *Framing effective practice: Topics and issues in the education of English language learners* (pp. 53–59). National Clearinghouse for Bilingual Education.

Arias, M. B., & Morillo-Campbell, M. (2008). *Promoting ELL parental involvement: Challenges in contested times* (ED506652). ERIC. http://eric.ed.gov/?id=ED506652

Baker, T. L. (2019). Reframing the connections between deficit thinking, microaggressions, and teacher perceptions of defiance. *Journal of Negro Education, 88*(2), 103–113.

Bandura, A. (2001). Social cognitive theory: An agentic perspective. *Annual Review of Psychology, 52*(1), 1–26.

Baron, A. S., Dunham, Y., Banaji, M., & Carey, S. (2014). Constraints on the acquisition of social category concepts. *Journal of Cognition and Development, 15*(2), 238–268.

Bell, C., Horn, B., & Roxas, K. (2007). We know it's service, but what are they learning? Preservice teachers' understanding of diversity. *Equity & Excellence in Education, 40*, 123–133.

Benson, J. E., & Johnson, M. K. (2009). Adolescent family context and adult identity formation. *Journal of Family Issues, 30*(9), 1265–1286. https://www.doi.org/10.1177/0192513X09332967

Berk, R. A. (2017). Microaggressions trilogy: Part 1. Why do microaggressions matter? *Journal of Faculty Development, 31*(1), 63–73.

Bertrand, M., Chugh, D., & Mullainathan, S. (2005). Implicit discrimination. *American Economic Review, 95*(2), 94–98.

Betancourt, H., & López, S. R. (1993). The study of culture, ethnicity, and race in American psychology. *American Psychologist, 48*, 629–637.

Bishop, R. S. (1990). Mirrors, windows, and sliding glass doors. *Perspectives, 1*(3), ix–xi.

Borrero, N., & Sanchez, G. (2017). Enacting culturally relevant pedagogy: Asset mapping in urban classrooms. *Teaching Education, 28*(3), 279–295.

Bracey, J. R., Bámaca, M. Y., & Umaña-Taylor, A. J. (2004). Examining ethnic identity and self-esteem among biracial and monoracial adolescents. *Journal of Youth & Adolescence, 33*(2), 123–132.

Branch, A. J. (2020). Promoting ethnic identity development while teaching subject matter content: A model of ethnic identity exploration in education. *Teaching and Teacher Education, 87*, 1–12. https://doi.org/10.1016/j.tate.2019.102918

Brewster, C., & Railsback, J. (2003). *Building trust with schools and diverse families: A foundation for lasting partnerships.* Northwest Regional Educational Laboratory.

Bryk, A., & Schneider, B. (2002). *Trust in schools: A core resource for improvement.* Russell Sage Foundation.

Call-Cummings, M., & Martinez, S. (2017). "It wasn't racism; it was more misunderstanding." White teachers, Latino/a students, and racial battle fatigue. *Race, Ethnicity and Education, 20*(4), 561–574.

Cameron, J. A., Alvarez, J. M., Ruble, D. N., & Fuligni, A. J. (2001). Children's lay theories about ingroups and outgroups: Reconceptualizing research on prejudice. *Personality and Social Psychology Review, 5*(2), 118–128.

Caraballo, L. (2019). Being "loud": Identities-in-practice in a figured world of achievement. *American Educational Research Journal, 56*(4), 1281–1317.

Carr, S. (2022, January 5). Public schools are struggling to retain Black teachers. These ex-teachers explain why. *Time.* time.com/6130991/black-teachers-resigning/

Chasey, K. (2013, September 19). 5 spotting techniques and rules everyone must know. *Breaking Muscle.* https://breakingmuscle.com/fitness/5-spotting-techniques-and-rules-everyone-must-know

Choi, J.-A. (2017). Why I'm not involved. *Phi Delta Kappan, 99*(3), 46–49.

Crenshaw, K. (1989). Demarginalizing the intersection of race and sex: A Black feminist critique of antidiscrimination doctrine, feminist theory and antiracist politics. *University of Chicago Legal Forum, 1*(8). http://chicagounbound.uchicago.edu/uclf/vol1989/iss1/8

DeAngelis, T. (2009, February). Unmasking "racial micro aggressions." *Monitor on Psychology, 40*(2). https://www.apa.org/monitor/2009/02/microaggression

Drago-Severson, E., & Blum-DeStefano, J. (2014). Leadership for transformational learning: A developmental approach to supporting leaders' thinking and practice. *Journal of Research on Leadership Education, 9*(2). https://doi.org/10.1177/1942775114527082

DyckFehderau, D., Holt, N. L., Ball, G. D., Alexander First Nation Community, & Willows, N. D. (2013). Feasibility study of asset mapping with children: Identifying how the community environment shapes activity and food choices in Alexander First Nation. *Rural and Remote Health, 13*(2289). https://era.library.ualberta.ca/items/94db564c-61a3-42a2-9227-49a2ed84de23/view/646987fd-1e8d-4a67-babd-16a721bca820/RRH_13_1_2289.pdf

Epstein, J. L. (2019). *School, family, and community partnerships: Your handbook for action* (4th ed.). Corwin.

Erikson, E. (1968). *Identity: Youth and crisis.* Norton.

Florence, M. (2017). *Stolen words* (Illustrated ed.). Second Story Press.

Gilliam, W. S., Maupin, A. N., Reyes, C. R., Accavitti, M., & Shic, F. (2016). *Do early educators' implicit biases regarding race and sex relate to behavioral expectations and recommendations for suspensions and expulsions?* Yale Child Study Center. https://medicine.yale.edu/childstudy/zigler/publications/Preschool%20Implicit%20Bias%20Policy%20Brief_final_9_26_276766_5379_v1.pdf

Girvan, E. J., Gion, C., McIntosh, K., & Smolkowski, K. (2017). The relative contribution of subjective office referrals to racial disproportionality in school discipline. *School Psychology Quarterly, 32*(3), 392–404.

Goddard, R., Tschannen-Moran, M., & Hoy, W. (2001). A multilevel examination of the distribution effects of teacher trust in students and parents in urban elementary schools. *The Elementary School Journal, 102*(1), 3–17.

Gorinski, R., & Fraser, C. (2006). *Literature review on the effective engagement of Pasifika parents and communities in education* (Pacific Islands School-Parent-Community Liaison). New Zealand Ministry of Education. http://www.educationcounts.govt.nz/publications/pasifika/5907

Greenwald, A. G., & Banaji, M. R. (1995). Implicit social cognition: Attitudes, self-esteem, and stereotypes. *Psychological Review, 102,* 4–27.

Greenwald, A. G., & Krieger, L. H. (2006). Implicit bias: Scientific foundations. *California Law Review, 94*(4), 945–967.

Gregory, A., & Roberts, G. (2017). Teacher beliefs and the overrepresentation of Black students in classroom discipline. *Theory Into Practice, 56*(3), 187–194.

Handy, D. J., Rodgers, K. B., & Schwieterman, T. A. (2011). Youth asset mapping: Showcasing youth empowerment and positive youth-adult partnership. *Journal of Family & Consumer Sciences, 103*(1), 9–15.

Harjo, J. (2000). *The good luck cat.* Houghton Mifflin Harcourt.

Helms, J. E. (2007). Some better practices for measuring racial and ethnic identity constructs. *Journal of Counseling Psychology, 54*(3), 235–246.

Hewstone, M., & Giles, H. (1997). Social groups and social stereotypes. In N. Coupland & A. Jaworski (Eds.), *Sociolinguistics* (pp. 270–283). Palgrave.

Hoy, W. K., & Tschannen-Moran, M. (2003). The conceptualization and measurement of faculty trust in schools: The Omnibus T-scale. In W. K. Hoy & C. G. Miskel (Eds.), *Studies in leading and organizing schools* (pp. 181–208). Information Age.

Hubbard, C. (2005). *Catching the moon.* Lee & Low Books.

Jones, B. (2020, September 22). *Reducing racism in schools: The promise of anti-racist policies* (Issue brief). Prepared by the University of Connecticut in affiliation with the Center for Education Policy Analysis. https://education.uconn.edu/2020/09/22/reducing-racism-in-schools-the-promise-of-anti-racist-policies/

Jones, N., Marks, R., Ramirez, R., & Ríos-Vargas, M. (2021, August 12). *Improved race and ethnicity measures reveal U.S. population is much more multiracial: 2020 Census illuminates racial and ethnic composition of the country.* U.S. Census Bureau. https://www.census.gov/library/stories/2021/08/improved-race-ethnicity-measures-reveal-united-states-population-much-more-multiracial.html

Kahneman, D. (2011). *Thinking, fast and slow.* Farrar, Straus and Giroux.

Kohli, R. (2009). Critical race reflections: Valuing the experiences of teachers of color in teacher education. *Race, Ethnicity and Education, 12,* 235–251.

Livingstone, J. (2014, January 29). Relatively speaking: Do our words influence how we think? *The Guardian.* https://www.theguardian.com/education/2014/jan/29/how-words-influence-thought

Logan, T. (2020, January 23). A brief history of black names, from Perlie to Latasha. *The Conversation.* https://theconversation.com/a-brief-history-of-black-names-from-perlie-to-latasha-130102

Lomotey, K., & Smith, W. A. (2023). *The racial crisis in American higher education: Continuing dilemmas, ongoing setbacks and new challenges* (3rd rev. ed.). SUNY Press.

Lucy, J. A. (1997). Linguistic relativity. *Annual Review of Anthropology, 26,* 291–312.

Malott, K. M., Paone, T. R., Schaefle, S., & Gao, J. (2015). Is it racist? Addressing racial microaggressions in counselor training. *Journal of Creativity in Mental Health, 10*(3), 386–398.

Marcia, J. (1980). Identity in adolescence. In J. Adelson (Ed.), *Handbook of adolescent psychology* (pp. 159–187). Wiley.

Mathews, S. M., & Savarimuthu, A. (2020, February). *Role of education in transmitting culture in society* [Conference paper]. https://www.researchgate.net/publication/339816271_Role_of_Education_in_Transmitting_Culture_in_Society

Miller, G. A. (1956). The magical number seven, plus or minus two: Some limits on our capacity for processing information. *Psychological Review, 63*(2), 81–97.

Miller-Cotto, D., & Byrnes, J. (2016). Ethnic/racial identity and academic achievement: A meta-analytic review. *Developmental Review, 41,* 51–70.

Morris, C. (2020, July 28). How to dismantle racism in the workplace: It starts at the top. *Forbes.* www.forbes.com/sites/carmenmorris/2020/07/28/how-to-dismantle-racism-in-the-workplace-it-starts-at-the-top/?sh=550a34b9bdcb

Mosca, J. F. (2017). *The girl who thought in pictures: The story of Dr. Temple Grandin.* The Innovation Press.

Muhammad, I. (2019). *The proudest blue.* Little, Brown Books for Young Readers.

Murphy, M. C., Steele, C. M., & Gross, J. J. (2007). Signaling threat: How situational cues affect women in math, science, and engineering settings. *Psychological Science, 18*(10), 879–885.

Nieto, S. (2002). *Language, culture, and teaching: Critical perspectives for a new century.* Lawrence Erlbaum Associates.

Nosek, B. A., Greenwald, A. G., & Banaji, M. R. (2005). Understanding and using the implicit association test: II. Method variables and construct validity. *Personality & Social Psychology Bulletin, 31*(2), 166–180.

Office of Educational Technology. (n.d.). *Learning.* U.S. Department of Education. https://tech.ed.gov/netp/learning/

O'Keefe, V. M., Wingate, L. R., Cole, A. B., Hollingsworth, D. W., & Tucker, R. P. (2015). Seemingly harmless racial communications are not so harmless: Racial microaggressions lead to suicidal ideation by way of depression symptoms. *The Official Journal of the American Association of Suicidology, 45*(5), 567–576.

Onikama, D., Hammond, O., & Koki, S. (1998, May). *Family involvement in education: A synthesis of research for Pacific educators.* Pacific Resources for Education and Learning.

Organisation for Economic Co-operation and Development. (2018). *The future of education and skills 2030: The future we want* [Position paper]. https://www.oecd.org/education/2030/E2030%20Position%20Paper%20(05.04.2018).pdf

Peña, P. A., & Duckworth, A. L. (2018). The effects of relative and absolute age in the measurement of grit from 9th to 12th grade. *Economics of Education Review, 66*, 183–190.

Penn State. (2017, July 28). *Discrimination creates racial battle fatigue for African-Americans.* www.psu.edu/news/campus-life/story/discrimination-creates-racial-battle-fatigue-african-americans/

Pew Research Center. (2015). *Multiracial in America: Proud, diverse, and growing in numbers.* https://www.pewsocialtrends.org/2015/06/11/chapter-2-counting-multiracial-americans/

Phinney, J. S. (1989). Stages of ethnic identity development in minority group adolescents. *Journal of Early Adolescence, 9*(1–2), 34–49.

Pierce, C., Carew, J., Pierce-Gonzalez, D., & Willis, D. (1978). An experiment in racism: TV commercials. In C. Pierce (Ed.), *Television and education* (p. 66). SAGE.

Pintrich, P. R. (2003). A motivational science perspective on the role of student motivation in learning and teaching contexts. *Journal of Educational Psychology, 95,* 667–686.

ReadWriteThink. (2005). *Oral history questions.* IRA/NCTE. http://www.readwritethink.org/files/resources/lesson_images/lesson805/questions.pdf

Renn, K. A. (2008). Research on biracial and multiracial identity development: Overview and synthesis. *New Directions for Student Services, 123,* 13–21.

Romero, L. S. (2018). The discipline gap: What's trust got to do with it. *Teachers College Record, 120*(11), 1–30.

Rydell, R. J., Van Loo, K. J., & Boucher, K. L. (2017). Stereotype threat: New insights into process and intervention. In A. J. Elliot, C. S. Dweck, & D. S. Yeager (Eds.), *Handbook of competence and motivation: Theory and application* (2nd ed., pp. 294–312). Guilford Press.

Scroggins, W. A., Mackie, D. M., Allen, T. J., & Sherman, J. W. (2016). Reducing prejudice with labels: Shared group memberships attenuate implicit bias and expand implicit group boundaries. *Personality & Social Psychology Bulletin, 42*(2), 219–229.

Shamir, L. (2020, February 3). A case against the STEM rush. *Inside Higher Ed.* https://www.insidehighered.com/views/2020/02/03/computer-scientist-urges-more-support-humanities-opinion

Shepherd, S., Owen, D., & Fitch, T. J. (2006). Locus of control and academic achievement in high school students. *Psychological Reports, 98*(2), 318–322.

Shih, M., Bonam, C., & Sanchez, D. (2007). The social construction of race: Biracial identity and vulnerability to stereotypes. *Cultural Diversity & Ethnic Minority Psychology, 13*(2), 125–133.

Silver, J. (Director). (1997). *A world of differences: Understanding cross-cultural communication* [Film]. Berkeley Media.

Singleton, G. E. (2021). *Courageous conversations about race* (3rd ed.). Corwin.

Skiba, R. J., Horner, R. H., Chung, C. G., Rausch, M. K., May, S. L., & Tobin, T. (2011). Race is not neutral: A national investigation of African American and Latino disproportionality in school discipline. *School Psychology Review, 40*(1), 85–107.

Smith, W., Hung, M., & Franklin, J. D. (2011). Racial battle fatigue and the miseducation of Black men: Racial microaggressions, societal problems, and environmental stress. *Journal of Negro Education, 80*(1), 63–82.

Solorzano, D., Ceja, M., & Yosso, T. (2000). Critical race theory, racial microaggressions, and campus racial climate: The experiences of African American college students. *Journal of Negro Education, 69*(1–2), 60–73.

Spencer, S. J., Steele, C. M., & Quinn, D. M. (1999). Stereotype threat and women's math performance. *Journal of Experimental Social Psychology, 35*(1), 4–28. https://doi.org/10.1006/jesp.1998.1373

Staats, C. (2016). Understanding implicit bias. *Education Digest, 82*(1), 29–38.

Starck, J. G., Riddle, T., Sinclair, S., & Warikoo, N. (2020). Teachers are people, too: Examining the racial bias of teachers compared to other American adults. *Educational Researcher, 49*(4), 273–284.

Steele, C. M., & Aronson, J. (1995). Stereotype threat and the intellectual test performance of African Americans. *Journal of Personality and Social Psychology, 69*(5), 797–811.

Steele, C. M., Spencer, S. J., & Aronson, J. (2002). Contending with group image: The psychology of stereotype and social identity threat. *Advances in Experimental Social Psychology, 34,* 379–440. https://doi.org/10.1016/S0065-2601(02)80009-0

Steiner, E. D., & Woo, A. (2021, June 14). *Job-related stress threatens the teacher supply: Key findings from the 2021 State of the U.S. Teacher Survey.* RAND Corporation. www.rand.org/pubs/research_reports/RRA1108-1.html

Sue, D. W. (2010). *Microaggressions and marginality: Manifestation, dynamics, and impact.* Wiley.

Sue, D. W., Capodilupo, C. M., & Holder, A. M. B. (2008). Racial microaggressions in the life experience of Black Americans. *Professional Psychology: Research and Practice, 39,* 329–336.

Sue, D. W., Capodilupo, C. M., Torino, G. C., Bucceri, J. M., Holder, A. M., Nadal, K. L., & Esquilin, M. (2007). Racial microaggressions in everyday life: Implications for clinical practice. *American Psychologist, 62*(4), 271–286.

Taylor, M. P. (2019, October 11). *Today's affinity groups: Risks and rewards.* Society for Human Resource Management. www.shrm.org/resourcesandtools/legal-and-compliance/employment-law/pages/affinity-groups-risks-rewards.aspx

Thomas, K., & Velthouse, B. (1990). Cognitive elements of empowerment: An "interpretive" model of intrinsic task motivation. *Academy of Management Review, 15,* 666–681.

Torres, L., Driscoll, M. W., & Burrow, A. L. (2010). Racial microaggressions and psychological functioning among highly achieving African-Americans: A mixed-methods approach. *Journal of Social and Clinical Psychology, 29*(10), 1074–1099.

Trumbull, E., Rothstein-Fisch, C., & Greenfield, P. (2000). *Bridging cultures in our schools: New approaches that work.* WestEd Knowledge Brief. http://wested.org/online_pubs/lcd-99-01.pdf

Valencia, R. R. (2010). *Dismantling contemporary deficit thinking: Educational thought and practice.* Routledge.

Villegas, A. M., & Lucas, T. (2002). Preparing culturally responsive teachers: Rethinking the curriculum. *Journal of Teacher Education, 53*(20), 20–32.

Weiss, H., Bouffard, S., Bridglall B., & Gordon, E. (2009). *Reframing family involvement in education: Supporting families to support educational equity.* Campaign for Educational Equity, Teachers College, Columbia University.

Welsh, R. O., & Little, S. (2018). The school discipline dilemma: A comprehensive review of disparities and alternative approaches. *Review of Educational Research, 88*(5), 752–794.

Zeiser, K., Scholz, C., & Cirks, V. (2018). *Maximizing student agency: Implementing and measuring student-centered learning practices.* American Institutes of Research.

Index

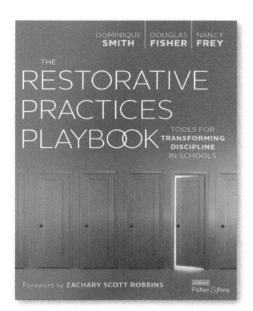

The Restorative Practices Playbook

Implementing restorative practices establishes a positive academic and social-emotional learning environment while building students' capacity to self-regulate, make decisions, and self-govern—the very skills students need to achieve. In this eye-opening, essential playbook, renowned educators Dominique Smith, Douglas Fisher, and Nancy Frey support educators with the reflection prompts, tools, examples, and strategies needed to create restorative practices.

The Social-Emotional Learning Playbook

Sparking deep reflection and transformative growth, this highly interactive playbook profiles six tenets of social and emotional learning—building resilience, belonging and prosocial skills, emotional regulation, relational trust and communication, individual and collective efficacy, and community of care. With this book in hand, jumpstart your social and emotional development journey, reduce compassion fatigue, and create alliances and opportunities for the children and adults in your school community to thrive.

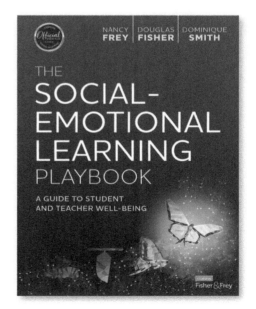

CORWIN Fisher & Frey

A SAGE Publishing Company

Helping educators make the greatest impact

CORWIN HAS ONE MISSION: to enhance education through intentional professional learning.

We build long-term relationships with our authors, educators, clients, and associations who partner with us to develop and continuously improve the best evidence-based practices that establish and support lifelong learning.